I BELIEVE IN DISCIPLESHIP

I Believe in Discipleship

The Adventure of Living

Rob Warner

Hodder & Stoughton

LONDON SYDNEY AUCKLAND

British Library Cataloguing in Publication Data
A record for this book is available from the British Library

ISBN 0 340 70985 5

Typeset by Avon Dataset Ltd, Bidford-on-Avon, Warks

Printed and bound in Great Britain by
the Guernsey Press Co. Ltd, Channel Isles

Hodder and Stoughton Ltd
A Division of Hodder Headline
338 Euston Road
London NW1 3BH

To everyone in 'Kairos – Church from Scratch'.
You are already teaching Claire and me so much
about the adventure and privilege
of whole-life discipleship.
Thank you so much.

We've only just begun . . .

Contents

Introduction

DISCIPLESHIP HAS OFTEN been the Christian Cinderella. Many churches offer 'discipleship classes' for new converts, which are no doubt often very helpful, but the clear implication is given that discipleship is to do with Christian beginnings. Once you complete your induction process, you are the finished article, a fully fledged disciple.

As soon as we turn to the New Testament we discover a very different understanding of discipleship. The Great Commission provides the climactic ending to Matthew's Gospel. The risen Christ delivers his marching orders to his Church. We are called to take the good news to the ends of the earth, making disciples of all peoples. New disciples need to be baptised and to be taught to put into practice everything that Christ taught on earth. And since he repeatedly affirmed the authority of the Old Testament, the Jewish Scriptures need to be included in the Christian Bible and discipleship training programmes. Jesus could not have been more clear. We are not instructed to make pew-sitters, sermon-tasters, worship-enjoyers or church-attenders. It is not enough for people to describe themselves as Christian or believers. Our task is to establish fully fledged disciples of Christ. They need to keep on growing in him, and so do we. And as we grow in the qualities of Christ, in our individual lives and in our relationships, we are also meant to keep on producing more disciples. The Church is meant to keep on growing in quality and in quantity. And effective disciple-making is crucial to this sustained vitality and growth.

Discipleship is about lifelong learning

In the New Testament, the word we translate as disciple means a 'learner'. In business today, there is much talk of learning organisations where there is a continuing commitment to review and development, both for individuals and the company. Learning is no longer thought to be complete when we leave full-time education or when we have been shown the ropes in our first week at work. Learning is for life.

Likewise, in the Gospels there is no graduation from Jesus' school of discipleship. Rabbis would teach their students both in theory and practice. Living close to your teacher meant you saw his wisdom expressed in his life. Discipleship was not like rote learning for an exam, assembling stockpiles of information for a brain dump in a schoolroom. Discipleship was a way of life: growth in understanding would be expressed in a developing lifestyle. To be a disciple is to be a learner, in theory and in practice, and there was always more for his first disciples to learn in the discipleship school of Jesus.

Discipleship is about lifelong following

At the heart of discipleship is not only a continuing opportunity to learn and to grow, but also a dedication to follow the Master. Matthew's Gospel, which was probably written as a manual of discipleship, repeatedly emphasises the importance of following Jesus (e.g. Matt. 4:20, 22, 25; 8:1, 23; 9:9, 27; 12:15; 14:13; 19:2, 28; 20:29, 34; 26:58; 27:55). This is Matthew's way of emphasising that we must always look to Jesus to lead the way. True discipleship is about following in the Master's footsteps. But the way of Jesus is never likely to be safe. It's about servanthood and faith, inviting us to take the risk and face the cost of putting others first. Discipleship is therefore a way of life that always requires of us new steps of faith and self-sacrifice.

True discipleship is whole-life discipleship

The old call to commitment has not lost its sting: 'If Jesus is not Lord of all, he is not Lord at all.' Discipleship means a complete, continuing and lifelong submission to the priorities of Christ. But this should never lead to a narrow, shallow, truncated and life-denying attitude. Jesus promised his followers life in all its fullness, but the Church has often preferred lots of religious meetings and committees instead. Life in all its fullness means learning how to make connections between Christ and every aspect of life. In the New Testament he is never locked up in a 'Sundays only' compartment. Our total experience of what it means to be human can be touched and enriched by Christ. Growth in discipleship means a growth into wholeness and integration, in our identity, our values and our total life experience.

The sheer breadth of the issues addressed in the Old Testament affirm that the totality of human existence and every field of enquiry and advance can be pursued in the service of God. The books of the law affirm public ethics, a moral code set in statutes, justice for all and protection for the poor. The history books interpret the present in the light of the past, while the prophetic books seek to interpret the present in the light of the future. The wisdom literature seeks to make sense of human existence from the accumulation of individual insights into the patterns and causal connections of daily life. The poetry in worship of the psalms encompasses every aspect of life and every emotional condition, from heights of joy to depths of despair. The great leaders of the Old Testament, from Moses to David to Ezra and Nehemiah, all demonstrate the fact that, in the hands of God, leaders can bring about remarkable change in the destiny of a nation: the socio-political arena is therefore unambiguously within the orbit of whole-life discipleship.

All human life is found in the Old Testament, and all fields of human endeavour not expressly prohibited by biblical morality can be pursued to the glory of God. Christian discipleship that is true to the Jewish Scriptures as well as the New Testament cannot but embrace the totality of life in the service of Christ. There is nothing narrowly religious, indifferent to the larger compass of life, to be found in the Bible. If our understanding of discipleship has not embraced this wider horizon, our narrowness may be a personal problem or a church hang-up, but the logic of biblical Christianity has always been nothing less than whole-life discipleship.

True discipleship is life-enriching

Christians sometimes get the impression that true discipleship is a fun-free zone. Some of those who are often being held up as shining examples of Christian dedication seem to have little time for laughter and the pleasures of life. They are so driven in their dedication that they tend to think of life's small pleasures more as distractions than gifts of God. Their religious devotion is far too intense to be able to take time to enjoy life. Not so Jesus: his first recorded miracle was to create more wine to help a wedding reception go well; he thoroughly enjoyed meals with friends and strangers; throughout his public ministry he set aside time to enjoy the company of his closest friends and followers; he was a superb storyteller, captivating the imagination of his audience and often using extravagant humour that could even be considered slapstick (think of the man with a plank sticking out of his eye); his pleasure in the beauty of creation is apparent when he speaks of the wild flowers of Galilee; and he even enjoyed a cooked breakfast in one of his resurrection appearances. Here is no pale Galilean, a wispy ascetic who is keen on prayer but indifferent to life. Jesus' zest for life positively bubbles over. To seek God first and live for his kingdom (Matt. 6:33) is not to lose touch with life, but to enter into life in all its fullness (John 10:10).

Here, then, is a clear, biblical framework for discipleship. It is for lifelong learners. It is for followers, not mere theorists, who will continue to put Jesus' ways into practice. It has implications for the whole of life, and not just a spiritual or religious zone. And it is designed to be life-enriching, bringing a deeper fulfilment, wholeness and fun to every aspect of human existence.

I invite you therefore not to undertake a course of study in discipleship, in a cold, theoretical way, but rather to enter an adventure of living; a journey of personal growth. And here is the paradox of the cross: the more we take the risk of living for others, the more personal fulfilment we shall know. Discipleship is not for beginners, so that eventually we can leave it behind. It's not for extremists and eccentrics, with an imbalanced view of life. Discipleship is for everyone, because Jesus Christ has offered us the most incredible gift. However rich or poor, powerful or powerless, well known or anonymous we may feel ourselves to be,

Christ has unlocked for us the possibilities of being as fully alive as we possibly can be. True discipleship promises nothing less than life to the full.

Some Christians are persuaded that there is only one model for discipleship growth, one structure of church, small group or 'circle of accountability' that everyone must adopt. I am not willing to be dogmatic where the Bible gives us flexibility, and I am not interested in developing a model of discipleship that only works within churches of a certain denomination, size or character. Much of my ministry crosses denominational boundaries, for example, this year I am speaking at national conferences organised by Baptists, Methodists, Assemblies of God, the Church of Scotland, and the United Free Church of Scotland. Discipleship is the inheritance of all Christians, and therefore this book is designed to help you grow in the life of faith, irrespective of your particular church context. Our calling as disciples is the same, even though the ways we put biblical teaching into practice may vary enormously.

This book makes no attempt to be exhaustive. I have begun a journey of exploration from some of the key signposts found in the Bible that take us into this adventuresome and open-ended way of living. In Part One, I have explored the larger framework of living as a servant of God, concentrating on the great themes of Genesis 1–3: appreciation of creation and care for the environment, work and wealth creation, male–female equality, the creation gift of marriage, the pursuit of scientific enquiry and artistic creativity, sin and fallenness. In Part Two, I have explored many of the great themes of the New Testament, focusing upon Paul's letter to the Colossians, in which he laid out his apostolic understanding of Christian maturity and whole-life discipleship.

I hope this book will be used in several ways: read by many individuals who want to 'get their act together' and fulfil their potential in Christ; studied in small groups, where discussion and prayer will help you put biblical discipleship into practice; and, as the basis for sermon series, to be read by the congregation week by week as the preachers tackle each theme in turn. My prayer is that this book will prove life-enriching for many disciples of Christ, both new and long-established.

I am so thankful for the privilege of being a part of 'Kairos –

Church from Scratch', where we share our lives together as a disciple-growing Church. I am also grateful to the many Christians over the years who have helped me understand discipleship better. Above all, my thanks, as always, go to my dear wife, Claire, and our sons, James and Tom: to share my life with them is a fantastic privilege and pleasure, even when I disappear from view to write another book or prepare for another conference.

Rob Warner
Summer 1999

Part One
Designer's Potential

Chapter 1

Caring for Creation

HI-FI SYSTEMS, KITCHEN appliances and computer software all have one thing in common – bulky manuals. The manufacturers make sure that the manuals spell out everything that their product can accomplish. But we don't read them; the vast majority of us just muddle through. Some think the best way to learn is by random experimentation. Others have had a bad experience in the past with a manual that was too technical or had been translated from Japanese with only partial success. Either way, the manuals gather dust on the shelf and we only refer to them if our washing machine packs up or our word processor flatly refuses to open or print our most important files.

Christians have always viewed the entire Bible as the Maker's instructions. More than a library of human reflections upon life and a compilation of close encounters with God, these are pages on which we encounter the 'something more' of divine revelation. The New Testament describes the Scriptures as 'God-breathed' (2 Tim. 3:16). That doesn't mean God dictated them word for word, but it does acknowledge a unique depth, authority and relevance to these books. One of the most astonishing and profound parts of the Old Testament is the story of creation in the first three chapters of Genesis. These ancient writings were composed in a pre-scientific, pre-technological world. The Middle East of that time was highly patriarchal and religious, so that the lives of ordinary people were dominated by powerful men and even more powerful superstitions. And yet, in these remarkable chapters, we can discover an extraordinary exploration of what it means to be fully human that totally transcends the limited horizon of the ancient world in which it was composed. God's breath upon these words means that they remain wonderfully relevant and applicable at the dawn of the third Christian millennium. Out of a society so very different from our own, there arose a glorious celebration of the wonders of creation and a timeless exploration, rich with enduring insights into the human condition. There can be no better place to begin our exploration of whole-life discipleship.

Because most of us never refer to the computer manuals, we never utilise more than a tiny fraction of the capabilities of our word processing software. It could do so much more for us, if only we took the trouble to learn. The potential stored on our hard drive is often much greater than the performance we know how to deliver. But to fulfil our potential as human beings, we need to begin with the Maker's intentions. The Bible is our manual for life, and here is one manual that we really do need to examine if we want to enjoy life to the full.

The song of creation

Everyone needs some space in their lives for awe and mystery. In Europe today there is a new quest for the spiritual, the transcendent, a sense of otherness beyond the narrow horizons of our daily concerns. Genesis 1 celebrates not only the glories of creation but also the Creator who composed the cosmic symphony. There is no attempt to be detached, offering an objective theory of the origins of life, for this poetic celebration refuses to separate description from praise. Far more than merely stating that creation owes its existence to the Creator, this is a hymn of praise, a celebration of the Creator's artistry.

Genesis 1 makes no attempt to set a date on creation. Nor does it explain the mechanisms by which God accomplished his work. What matters is that the origin of life is not some cosmic accident. The opening phrase – 'In the beginning, God created . . .' (Gen. 1:1) – is not an argument for God's existence, but a declaration that God is the starting point for all things. He is self-existent: everything else ultimately depends upon God for its coming into being, but God has no external reference point. God just *is*. This sets God apart from creation in a mysterious, transcendent otherness. The source of life is quite separate from the cosmos he has shaped.

The first chapter of Genesis is built around two refrains. At the beginning of each stage of creation, God speaks out and his authoritative word brings life into being. At the end of most, but not all, stages, God reviews his work in progress and decrees that it is good. There is no implication that some stages of creation were not quite so good. This variation is typical of this sophisticated poem, where the repetition is elegant yet restrained.

God's appreciation of creation is echoed by the poet-writer of Genesis. There is evident pleasure taken in the particular beauties of each stage of creation. As the picture builds up, we are presented with a cosmos that is full of variety and delight, as orderly as it is beautiful. The poet invites us both to enjoy the splendours of creation and to respond to them at depth, experiencing creation's beauty as the craftsmanship of God. It is also clear that God continues to be involved as his creative work unfolds at each stage of creation. God's pleasure is as constant as his artistry. There is no suggestion of creation as a passing whim of the Creator, something with which God might soon become bored.

These great themes of God the Creator are taken up later in the Bible. He is the Lord of all creation (Ps. 24:1–2). There is a song expressed by the cosmos, in which all things declare the glory of God (Ps. 19:1–4). The distinctive qualities of each element of creation, from the soaring majesty of mountains to the exquisite harmonies of songbirds, all contribute to the cosmic symphony of praise. There is a revelation built into our experience of creation, which speaks of God's majestic otherness and goodness (Job 38–9). Creation's grandeur invites us to keep a sense of perspective about ourselves: despite our egocentricity, the cosmos has been fashioned for the glory of God rather than solely for the benefit of humankind.

Men, women and creation

Modern urban living inevitably tends to cut us off from the seasonal cycles and the immensity of creation. We are losing touch with the natural world. Life becomes a nine to five routine, irrespective of the time of year. Supermarkets provide us with an uninterrupted supply of fruit and vegetables, flying them in from whichever part of the world they are in season at any particular time of year. Urban living is the reason why many city dwellers experience a sense of well-being after a day in the countryside and why others feel compelled to look at mountains or oceans at regular intervals. We are created as beings who respond to the immensity of creation and who need a sense of the transcendent – a level of reality beyond the humdrum routines and pressures of our everyday lives. I'm sure that this quest for ultimate reality is behind the current spiritual reawakening in Western Europe, where many young people who are totally bored with established religion are looking for some kind of authentic spiritual awareness and encounter.

Genesis 1–3 not only speaks about creation and its origins in God; these chapters also explore our connections as human beings with both the Creator and his handiwork. The poet in Genesis makes no attempt to provide a date for the origin of Homo sapiens, but emphasises that our existence came about by purpose, not chance. Human existence is more complex than the rest of creation. On the one hand, we are created in a similar way to everything else. God spoke and human beings were created, just like the birds, fish and mammals (Gen. 1:26). We are constructed from 'the dust' (Gen. 2:7) – that is, from the same physical building blocks as the rest of the cosmos. On the other hand, we are a special creation, requiring direct intervention. This is emphasised in four ways. First, our creation is so significant that the last stage of creation is set aside specifically for humankind. Second, unlike any other creatures, we are said twice to be made 'in God's image' (Gen. 1:26, 27) – a theme to which we will return in Chapter 3. Third, in addition to taking the dust, God breathes life into our nostrils (Gen. 2:7). This suggests a distinction between us and other carbon life forms: we have self-awareness, the capacity to shape our own future through our choices, and we have been fashioned as spiritual beings, made to worship and pray to the Creator. Fourth, we are appointed 'over' the natural world: able to harness the earth's resources for our own benefit. In short, we have a continuity with the rest of creation, and also a discontinuity. We are a part of the created cosmos, and yet distinct from it, as spiritual beings made in the image of God.

Custodians of creation

For the last hundred years, the big controversy around Genesis 1 has been whether it is compatible with the theory of evolution. Some have argued that evolution rules out Genesis 1; others have argued that Genesis 1 rules out evolution. I cannot help but feel that the original poet would have been mystified by the controversy: his emphasis was not on *how* God did it, but the fact that creation owes its existence to God. This means that the beauty and order we can enjoy in creation point beyond themselves to the splendour of their Creator. The great risk is that, in reducing the theology of Genesis 1 to a crude yes/no with regard to evolution, we will almost certainly end up missing many of the themes that are actually centre stage in this great hymn of creation.

Men and women are called to subdue and rule the earth. God invites us to provide for ourselves from nature's larder, and also promises continued provision for other creatures, maintaining the supply of their food stocks. This speaks of humankind's freedom and responsibility. We have the opportunity to cultivate crops and mine for natural resources, to harness the world's natural resources and to develop new technologies. There is no suggestion in Genesis that the best thing we could do is to abandon all technology and go back to nature in a primitive simplicity. We are entitled to enjoy the fruits of creation and the benefits of our own innovations. However, we remain accountable to God. The world is given over to our use, but in trust and with certain strings attached. When the world came into our hands it was very good, and God expects us to take excellent care of his glorious work of art. That means respecting bio-diversity, protecting natural habitats, preventing wanton pollution and preserving the beauty of the earth.

The New Testament explains that men and women have subjected creation to futility (Rom. 8:20). The whole earth pays a very great price for our fallenness. At our best, we can enhance the song of creation. At our worst, we are like the boy in a school choir who is tone deaf and growls his way through every song, even causing those sitting near him to sing out of tune as well. Though the whole of creation was designed to express a symphony of praise, we are the discordant voice. When we tear down rain forests, cover the countryside in ever more motorways, turn cows into carnivores by feeding them flesh (which almost certainly led to the disaster of BSE and CJD), and engage in intensive farming practices that over-stress animals and strip them of their dignity and worth, we are the disruptors of creation's natural balance. When Paul spoke of the longing of creation (Rom. 8:19–21), this is not only a longing on our behalf – that men and women might enter into the fullness of resurrection life in Christ – it also seems to be a longing on behalf of creation itself, that the Creator's original order and harmony might one day be restored. Like graffiti on a Michelangelo, human excesses have grossly disfigured the beauty of creation.

Creation prejudices

Christians have often been guilty of destructive attitudes towards creation. The early Church and Western Christianity have often been overly and unconsciously influenced by Greek philosophy, and in particular by the quite brilliant writings of Plato. There is a dualism at the heart of Platonic thinking. Life is split into two levels: the lower level of material existence, where everything is subject to change, and the higher level of spiritual existence and reason, where everything is changeless and constant. This way of looking at life is quite unlike the Judaeo-Christian perspective of the Bible, where there is a wholeness and an integration in human existence.

Platonic dualism can infect Christian thinking in several ways. First, it can lead us to suppose that all that really matters is the spiritual aspect of life, and the rest is mere distraction. This is seen in many ways: the medieval suspicion that marriage makes you less spiritual; the traditional Western prayer posture that requires us to put our bodies and senses into neutral, kneeling with hands to-gether and eyes closed; the modern suspicion that any concern for creation is really New Age rather than Christian.

Second, it can lead to a truncated gospel, in which all that matters is our personal conversion and eternal destiny in heaven with Christ: Christians have sometimes ended up with a doctrine of redemption that has cut loose from a doctrine of creation. When I was first converted we sang 'this world is not my home'. There's a measure of truth in that, of course, because we live in the confidence of our resurrection hope. But such attitudes are less than fully biblical, because they promote an other-worldly indifference to life on earth. Heavenly minded Christians have often been of little use on earth.

Third, this dualism can lead to what I call an 'end-times indifference'. During Ronald Reagan's time as President of the United States he appointed a self-professed born-again Christian to a position that granted national responsibility for the environment. At one time this man declared that he had no obligation to protect the environment for future generations since Jesus was coming again soon. Let me state as bluntly as possible that there is no possible biblical justification for such an attitude of wanton exploitation and despoliation of the environment. If the earth is the Lord's, we are accountable to him for the way we care for it. If the earth declares the glory of God, we have a responsibility not to diminish that cosmic symphony of praise by acts of environmental vandalism.

While these various prejudices have sometimes infected Christians, mainly as a result of a misplaced and unbiblical dualism that denigrates the material in an attempt to elevate the spiritual, Genesis 1 also stands as a corrective to two other unhelpful attitudes. The first is worshipping creation itself, rather than the Creator. Whether in worshipping Mother Earth or worshipping the pagan deities, whether in pantheism (everything is in God) or in panentheism (God is in everything), when the biblical distinction between God and his creation is lost we begin to worship created things. Time after time the Old Testament law and prophets railed against such tendencies. To appreciate the splendours of creation is natural, but worship must be reserved for the Creator God alone, whose existence depends on no external factors and who lives in an eternal present moment, from before he brought creation and time to their first dawn.

The second unhelpful attitude is to abandon any sense of a hierarchy of values. We have seen that some Christians, along with the rest of the Western industrial and post-industrial society, have sometimes made their hierarchy of values too extreme, so that the natural world hardly matters at all. In revolt against this attitude, which has led to the rape of the planet, some are now divinising other life forms at the expense of human dignity. A few years ago, a puma in California attacked and killed a jogger. The jogger was a single parent, and a spontaneous collection was started to raise funds for her children. The puma clearly needed to be destroyed, before it turned more joggers into its regular meat supply, but when it was killed, its young cubs needed to be rescued and so a second spontaneous collection was started. More money was raised for the young pumas than the young humans. This suggests, at least to me, a breakdown in values: pumas certainly do matter within the great scheme of creation, but humans ultimately matter more.

Green Christians

If we worship the Creator God, the way we treat creation becomes an act of worship. This is true in our appreciation of creation: we need to make space to enjoy its splendour and be enriched by the sense of God's grandeur that is so eloquent in the majesty of an unspoiled landscape. It is also true in our attitude to ecology and recycling. Internationally, Christians need to promote concern for the environment – for example, encouraging financial incentives for developing countries to resist the understandable temptation to take ecological short-cuts for the sake of economic development that could have potentially devastating consequences. Nationally, churches should be encouraging such policies as the wise steward-ship of non-renewable natural resources, the urgent development of post-car transportation policies, and restrictions on intensive farming. Locally, churches should be taking a lead in practical initiatives, avoiding non-recyclable products, applauding cosmetics companies that refuse to test their products on animals, and pro-viding recycling bins for the local community. Don't leave it to someone else: according to the Bible, all Christians are called to be 'green Christians'.

Many churches in Britain still celebrate the harvest festival. This service was reputedly invented by a nineteenth-century Anglican, concerned that industrialisation was taking people away from the land. In many urban settings the event has become detached from the realities of today's world, a once-a-year escape into an agricul-tural nostalgia. It's good to give thanks to God for the harvest, but we need to reclaim a much broader canvas of thankfulness for creation itself. I would love to see more churches developing a celebration of Creation Sunday. This would combine a celebration of the splendours of creation with an acceptance of our practical responsibilities as stewards of God's planet. A multimedia celebration, including photos and paintings, dance and music, video clips and banners could lift our spirits so much more richly than simply seeing little Jimmy carry an oversize turnip or a tin of baked beans to the front of the church. A local church could even publish a charter of realistic, practical steps to demonstrate our care for creation. Non-churchgoers also recognise the transcendent beauty of creation and the need for our society to become more responsible, so these initiatives could even have an evangelistic impact. But the primary motive is worship. Whole-life discipleship is bound to encompass both appreciating creation and taking better care of the natural world. The God we serve is the Creator of all, and we honour his name by pursuing a positive and responsible approach towards the eco-system of planet Earth.

Chapter 2

The Gift and Curse of Work

JESUS SPENT MORE years as a carpenter than as a preacher, and there's certainly no suggestion in the New Testament that his carpentry years were wasted years. It's time that Christians escaped once and for all from the prejudice that implies there are two kinds of Christian, with the result that those whose work is anything but 'full-time Christian work' are somehow doomed to be second-best in the spiritual league table.

Blessing and curse

Genesis 1–3 invites us to see work from two quite different perspectives, both as a gift of God and as a curse. Work begins with God himself. Genesis 1 presents a God who is at work, actively involved in bringing his creation to fruition. To be made in the image of a working God is to be made for work. We are active and achieving even as God is active and achieving. It is satisfying and fulfilling to accomplish something with our lives, to harness our energies to fulfil targets, to make something happen that would have been impossible without effort and focus. This positive view of work as a divine gift is reinforced in Genesis 2:15, where Adam is set in the Garden of Eden expressly to 'work it and take care of it'. Effort, productivity and responsibility are combined in this divine gift. We were made to work, and work was designed to give us a sense of satisfaction and fulfilment.

Some Christians affirm work in the caring professions, but are not so sure about commerce and the profit motive. This modern Christian prejudice has no biblical justification. In creation, God creates out of nothing, which is surely a mandate for wealth creation in the world of business. Healthy financial results can express something very positive of what it means to be created in the image of a working God. In Britain, Christians are also likely to be influenced by a general and widespread prejudice – which Tony Blair has described as a 'certain snobbery against those who set out to make money'. According to the Scriptures, reflected both in the Jewish tradition and the Protestant work ethic, entrepreneurs can be effective Christian disciples just as much as those in the caring and education professions.

The downside of work is spelt out in Genesis 3:17–19. After the Fall, part of God's judgement on the human race concerns work. The ground will be cursed, thorns and thistles will multiply, and human work will be marked by 'painful toil' and 'the sweat of your brow'. Fulfilment through work can be degraded into the drudgery of hard labour. The job satisfaction of the Garden of Eden now gets spoiled by the Monday morning feeling. Work itself is not God's judgement: our capacity for work and the fulfilment it can give us are privileges of creation. But work is now two-faced in our experience: it comes to us both as a gift and as a curse.

Work and identity

In the United Kingdom there are two standard questions you face when you meet someone for the first time: 'What's your name?' and 'What do you do?' For many Americans there's often a third question that Brits hardly ever ask directly – 'How much do you make?' These questions underline the fact that our work is an integral part of our identity. That's why change at work is often difficult to take.

Redundancy makes the statement that we are no longer needed in a particular workplace, for reasons of reorganisation or a decline in the company's fortunes. But for many it is felt as a more fundamental rejection that corrodes their sense of self-worth. Retirement can do the same, which is why enlightened companies now invest in pre-retirement training, and even counselling. For some, retirement has become a new dawn of opportunities for personal development. But for others it still carries connotations of being 'put on the scrap heap'; not doing productive labour in the workplace can result in feelings of having no intrinsic worth. Such people often don't live long beyond their date of retirement.

Stripped of paid work, their lives lack purpose and direction and they seem to lose interest in life itself.

Some men now face an unfamiliar crisis if their wife's career takes off faster than their own. While some men are able to admire their partner's achievements and enjoy their share of the material benefits, others struggle with their own sense of identity. When men have been brought up to assume that they will always be the main or sole breadwinner, the sexual revolution in the job market can leave them struggling to sustain their self-worth: 'If I cannot even be the main breadwinner, what use am I?'

Some women who have chosen not to take on paid employment outside the home can experience a similar usurpation of their role if their partner is made redundant or retires. One explained to me, 'The home has always been mine during the day, to clean as I choose and to enjoy as I choose. Now I feel as if my husband is trespassing upon my private space. I have no tasks or time to call my own any more!'

Our society is facing the biggest transition the workplace has ever known. In pre-industrial societies, most people had no choice at all about their work. Women would almost always run the home, come what may. And sons would usually carry on their father's business. The industrial age brought about new opportunities to break free from the family's traditional field of work. People were no longer automatically defined by their father's trade ('I come from a long line of bakers'), but became increasingly free to enjoy their individual choices and achievements ('I am a solicitor'). Although there was a dramatic shift from the family to the individual, an underlying assumption remained constant: for almost everyone, once you had entered a field of work, you would continue there until your death or retirement.

The rate of change in the workplace has exploded. Whole departments can be replaced by computers. Skills that have been long cherished are now becoming obsolete. No one can take it for granted that they will still be working for the same company in twenty years' time. This new volatility in employment is expressed in many ways: companies that used to reward long-service now choose to offload their older staff first in a time of redundancies; individuals no longer retain the traditional sense of company loyalty, but take it for granted that in due course they will probably need to move on; contracts in many fields of work are increasingly short-term rather than open-ended; those in high-paid employment often make plans to retire as early as possible; and an increasing number are working from home in a portfolio of part-time projects. Whereas once we took on a field of work for life – once a banker, always a banker – young adults in Western Europe today must expect to retrain during their working lives for perhaps as many as three or four different careers.

These rapid transitions are beginning to have a profound impact upon our sense of identity and self-worth. Most of us can no longer take it for granted that our first career will be an essential part of who we are until we retire. This can reinforce a kind of hyper-individualism: I'm busy looking after myself, and everyone else will have to learn to do the same. But it can also open up more profound questions about who we are and what life is really for.

At the same time, our society is tending to reduce everything to its cash value. 'If it don't make money,' one Texas billionaire decreed, 'it ain't pretty!' This narrow consumerism can grievously undermine the self-worth of those who are long-term unemployed or trying to live on the minimum state pension. It is also reflected in the apologetic response some people make when asked what they do – 'Oh, I'm *just* a housewife.' Here is a remarkable reversal in the value attached to a role. Two generations ago, it was more or less automatic that young women would give up work when they got married, investing their lives in home-making and child-rearing. Looked at positively, the role was esteemed highly. Looked at negatively, it was imposed as an almost universal straitjacket.

Today, increasing numbers of women go out to work and many take a fairly short time out when their children are very young. The reason for the new tone of apology attached to staying at home is at least in part because it has no cash value. We need therefore to emphasise that Genesis speaks of us being created as working beings without any regard to pay. Those who have taken time out from paid work to care for children or for seriously ill relatives, women and men alike, are just as worthy of esteem as those whose work comes with all the benefits of a high salary.

Christian identity is founded upon God's saving love: my self-worth and identity are not ultimately based upon my job, my salary and my achievements, but rather upon Christ's saving grace at the cross and my new status as a beloved and adopted child in the family of God. That doesn't mean that Christians are immune to the pressures of job insecurity, unemployment and redundancy. But it does mean that our work identity is set within a larger canvas.

A society that is losing touch with the once nearly universal experience of a job for life will be increasingly filled with people who need to look elsewhere for a settled sense of self. The more we can develop a sense of our identity as disciples of Christ, secure in eternal love, the more attractive the gospel will become in a world where the shelf-life of our work identities is getting shorter all the time.

Work and rest

Rest is becoming a scarce commodity in the Western world. The world is seen differently on foot: once you get behind the wheel of a car, the slightest hold-up is frustrating. A business trip to the United States once included a leisurely holiday on board ship. Now we fly out on the day of a transatlantic business meeting and hit the ground running. It's the same with cooking and computers: we become impatient with the seconds it takes for our microwave to finish cooking or our computer to finish printing. As an African once observed, 'You have the clocks, but we have the time.' Recent evidence suggests that the British are now surviving on an hour's less sleep than their parents' generation as we try to squeeze more and more into our working days. Life gets subdivided into ever smaller sections of time, and every millisecond counts.

Most of us say we work in order to live, but our schedules suggest that a growing number end up living in order to work. There is always another deadline, another crisis, another unexpected pressure. Sometimes an employer is taking advantage, always coming up with another excuse to squeeze in some extra hours. Sometimes we are self-driven. Maybe we have perfectionist tendencies. Maybe we are trying to fulfil impossible expectations. Maybe we don't know how to say no. Or maybe we find our work so fulfilling we just don't know when or how to stop.

I remember the first time I entered a three-mile race – I was used to sprinting and so set off at completely the wrong speed! We have to learn to pace ourselves, not only in athletics, but also in life. I remember a head teacher talking with me about the difference between his first and second posts as head: 'At my first school, I did far too much in the first year. By the time I was exhausted, everyone else expected me to be able to keep up that impossible pace all the time. In my second school, I took on a workload at the beginning that I could realistically sustain. It was a much healthier experience for everyone involved.'

We are made in the image of a God who works and rests. God has no need to rest, which suggests that he rested in the seventh epoch of creation for our sake, since rest is an unavoidable human requirement. For a short period of time we can work to a high level of intensity. Sooner or later it's payback time, when our bodies demand that we make up for our energy overdraft. If we don't look after ourselves with enough time out for sleep and rest, our bodies will start to lodge their complaints more and more forcefully. When we're too busy to rest, we're too busy.

Rest is about more than collapsing exhausted into bed. At the end of each stage of creation, God paused to appreciate what he had accomplished. This suggests a creative interconnection between work and play. Times of recreation enrich our lives and make us more productive in the workplace, just as hard work makes times of rest so much more satisfying. We often speak of a holiday as a 'well-earned rest'. Some people who are long-term unemployed struggle to keep a sense of shape and discipline to their lives: without the demands of work, open-ended opportunities to rest and play become unfocused and unrewarding. The plays of Shakespeare and the music of Mozart represent the high points of their cultures: for the dramatist and composer, their creations were doubtless hard work, but those who are truly enriched by their works must enjoy them as leisure pursuits. They cannot possibly be fully appreciated when they are treated merely as opportunities for corporate hospitality, a different venue for doing deals.

The Ten Commandments are listed twice in the Old Testament (Exod. 20; Deut. 5). The most significant variation is found in the fourth commandment, which calls for a work-free day every week.

In Exodus, the emphasis is upon a holy day; in Deuteronomy, it's about observing a day of rest. Here we see two complementary ways of emphasising the value of time away from paid work. First, there is need to make space to offer worship to God, making sure that living faith is not squeezed out by the intensity of our work schedule. Second, there is the need to take time out, for the sake of family, friends and leisure interests, so that our total life experience does not become narrowed down to the horizons of our working life, interrupted only by a few snatched hours of sleep.

The disciple at work

We have seen that work has intrinsic value because God has made us with a built-in capacity for work. The New Testament underlines this principle by instructing Christian slaves to work as if their master was Christ himself (Eph. 6:5–6). The first way in which we witness effectively is by doing our job to the best of our ability. Sadly, there are some Christians who have a reputation for being unproductive workers. They are too busy praying or witnessing during working hours to get the job done well and on time. The Bible gives us no excuse for such behaviour.

Just as Christian employees have an obligation to work hard, Christian employers have a duty to treat their staff well and pay them fairly. The Old Testament prophets were tireless in denouncing the public piety of the powerful in Israel, who were faithful in temple worship while exploiting the poor: '. . . on the day of your fasting, you do as you please and exploit all your workers' (Isa. 58:3). Such religion is empty and worthless. If a committed Christian is zealous on Sundays but unscrupulously exploits their staff midweek, God is not fooled. Whole-life discipleship means giving full and faithful expression to Christian values in every aspect of our lives:

> Is not this the kind of fasting I have chosen:
> to loose the chains of injustice
>   and untie the cords of the yoke,
> to set the oppressed free
>   and break every yoke? (Isa. 58:6)

Work must be a place of integrity, for employers and employees alike. The prophet Amos specifically brought God's word of judgement against crooked weights and measures in the market. In a similar way, the Christian disciple will need to opt out of the conventional dishonesties of some companies: the promise that the cheque is in the post when it isn't; the inflation of expenses; unreasonable delays in paying bills. We also face an obligation to be a 'whistle blower' in extreme cases of illegality and corruption. Some organisations attempt to demand an absolute loyalty from their employees. Just as Jesus instructed his followers to render to Caesar what is Caesar's, and to God what is God's, we must render to our employer a hard day's work. However, our reliability will always be set within the larger context of our absolute and uncompromising loyalty to the standards of Christ.

Work is an arena where relationship temptations are common. When I was a publisher I attended one secular conference where the story was that almost everyone was 'bed-hopping'. As a student, I took a job on campus as a cleaner one summer. The regular cleaners were shocked by a visiting conference of chartered accountants, who were much more sexually voracious than the full-time students. The boundaries are obvious between a good working relationship with a colleague and the emotional preparations for adultery. If we are going out of our way to spend time with a particular individual nearly every day, if we are confiding in them more than our marriage partner, or if we are comparing them favourably with our partner and complaining to them about our partner's deficiencies, the alarm bells should start ringing very loudly indeed.

When Jesus called us the 'salt of the earth' (Matt. 5:13), he was inviting us to be spread out as an influence for good, rather than encouraging us to stay huddled together in the salt cellar. The front line troops of Christian witness need to be confident when they go out to work on Monday morning that they are taking the Spirit of Christ with them. Many of us spend more time at work than in any other aspect of our lives. Work is therefore the place of our greatest witnessing opportunities. This is particularly so for those of us who live in cities, where we may have little time or opportunity to get beyond a nodding acquaintance with our neighbours. In the eyes of the people who see us at work from Monday to Friday, our daily lifestyle will commend or undermine the good news of Christ far more than any direct words of witness. Above all, we must emphasise that our Christian distinctiveness needs to be essentially positive. Certainly, there are specific things a Christian should not do, but what characterised Jesus was *positive holiness*. The Pharisees *avoided* wrongdoing, but Jesus went the extra mile, put others first, and lived in such a way that every individual was given respect and experienced the benefits of his self-giving love. If we are noticed only for the things we *don't* do, our Christian witness is woefully deficient.

Some of the best evangelistic services at which I have spoken have been organised in the workplace, including a government department carol service in a conference room and another for the head offices of a number of building societies and retailing organisations. I spoke two years running for one hospital Christian Union. The second time they were very apologetic because they had been unable to book the hospital chapel. As a result, the Christmas event took place in the room next to the student bar. People who had no intention of attending a carol service dropped in to see what was going on, with a beer in one hand and a cigarette in the other. As far as I was concerned, it was fantastic – much more like Jesus' proclamation than being tucked away out of sight in a chapel.

Work should never be seen as a distraction from the 'real business' of Christian living. If you are in work, then your workplace can be seen as a place of Christian service and witness, and your work itself as a gift of God. Whole-life discipleship is not locked into Christian meetings, but embraces every aspect of life. Made in the image of a working God, we experience work as both a blessing and a curse, and we are called to express the life and values of Christ in our workplace. Made in the image of a God who rested from his work of creation, we are called to maintain a healthy balance in our lives, neither shirking hard work nor working so singlemindedly that we never have time for relationships or recreation. No one ever expressed the death-bed regret, 'I wish I'd spent more time at the office!' Home life, church commitments and leisure opportunities all too easily get treated as Any Other Business on the Agenda of Life. The Christian disciple is called to work diligently, but we should also be able to demonstrate that there is a good deal more to life than work.

Chapter 3

Women and Men in the Image of God

MEDIEVAL PAINTINGS OF the temptation of Adam and Eve developed a tradition of giving two of the characters the same face. Not Adam and Eve, but Eve and the serpent. A male-dominated society wanted to blame the woman as much as possible for the Fall. Adam was in the image of God, but Eve was in the image of Satan.

Such paintings provide a telling insight into the attitudes of medieval Europe, but have no justification for their portraiture in Genesis 1–3. Even more startling is the fact that theologians reinforced a similar anti-women prejudice. Some early Church Fathers suggested that only males are made in the image of God, whereas women are the second, subordinate and derivative gender. Just as in twentieth-century apartheid in South Africa, we find Christians with social status grievously distorting the Bible in order to justify a deeply rooted prejudice in their society against another people group.

Genesis 1:27 is quite emphatic. Men and women are both made in the image of God – and equally so. There is no hierarchy of genders, no suggestion that one gender is in any sense superior. This is astonishingly radical within an ancient, patriarchal society. But it is unambiguous. In the creation mandate there is an absolute equality of persons, irrespective of gender.

So does this mean that there are no differences between men and women at all, beyond the obvious ones of plumbing and body mass? It is notoriously difficult to distinguish between intrinsic, sexual differences – that is, what is built into the male and female of the species – and gender expectations – that is, what is expected as masculine and feminine behaviour in different societies. To illustrate gender expectations, if a Victorian lady of high social status heard the word 'blood', she was expected to swoon help-lessly, while an Amazonian female warrior would spring into action, seizing her weapons in response to this delicious call to arms.

Sexual stereotyping pushes to extremes the contrast between male and female responses, but we can trace some underlying differences. Girls, for example, not only mature more quickly during adolescence, but they also tend to develop earlier in primary education both in reading and mathematics. Women also tend to cultivate a richer vocabulary to reveal their inner life, whereas men's conversation is often more detached and self-protecting – who should have won the World Cup rather than how I am feeling about myself. This contrasting use of language can lead to some common misunderstandings. Elaine Storkey tells the story of a couple who take turns to do the weekly shopping. One week the man makes the trip, and she asks, 'Where did you buy the fish?' He interprets this as a direct enquiry for informa-tion and replies, 'Tesco's'. Next week, she makes the trip and he asks the same question, 'Where did you buy the fish?' She interprets this as a veiled complaint and replies, 'Why? What's wrong with it?'

While there are built-in differences, men and women are not as different as we once supposed. In the nineteenth century, there were concerted efforts to protect women from the demands of higher education. The fear was that university learning would prove too exacting for the frailties of the female brain and body. Some feared traumatic consequences such as mental breakdown or the failure of the reproductive system if the female brain was overtaxed with study. Today in Britain a gender deficit *has* opened up in the classroom, particularly in GCSE and A level exams. But now it is the boys who are failing to keep up, with their results increasingly lagging behind the girls'.

What's happened in academic study is paralleled in sport. The last forty years have seen a steady increase in the number of athletic events in which women have been entitled to compete. At one time it was feared that women would be unable to take part safely in long distance running. Step by step, the prejudice has been rolled back, so that women can now compete at every distance from 100 metres to the marathon, even though top male athletes can run faster than top female athletes over all the distances in current competition. In the 1990s, a team of sport scientists evaluated the weight/strength/stamina ratio of male and female athletes to determine whether women could ever run faster than men. Their conclusion was that if a double-length marathon was organised as a mixed event, women would win every time.

Here is a great irony: there are irreducible differences between the male and female physique, but it is actually the women who have the greater stamina over long distances. The generations of athletics' regulators who attempted to protect women through restricting the distances they were allowed to run were not in reality legislating in the light of intrinsic sexual differences, but were instead imposing on women an arbitrary gender expectation.

It's hard to tell where innate differences end and gender expectations take over. Adults treat a baby differently depending on whether it's dressed as a boy or a girl. In American studies, the 'boy baby' was bounced vigorously and given toys that need to be bashed, such as large, plastic hammers. The 'girl baby' was held gently, talked to in a soothing way, and given soft toys to cuddle. Since the same baby was involved, the adult behaviour was mainly determined not by their response to the particular child's responses, but rather by their own gender expectations. So when a girl plays with dolls rather than guns, is that an innate female preference or is it an imposed gender expectation? In all probability, many such preferences reflect a complex interaction between sexual differences and cultural expectations.

In June 1998, *The Times* reported the emergence of a new consensus about the qualities needed for tomorrow's successful leaders in business. They will need to understand team-building, juggling roles and working collaboratively. Their staff will expect them to be more co-operative and less authoritarian than the previous generation of company bosses. Many look at this range of skills for tomorrow's leaders and conclude that women may be more adept than men at working in these ways. If these are indeed the qualities that women are more likely to bring to leadership, then I for one say bring on the women! Just as the old manual worker has lost his place in the workforce, now the construction of delicate micro-circuitry has replaced heavy labour and brute force, the old macho tyrant of the boardroom may also be edging towards the eve of extinction.

Since God made human persons in two genders, we can affirm a distinction between male and female, even if some of the differences are not quite as clear as our society once thought. At the same time, we must affirm that men and women are made equally in the image of God. So *vive la différence et vive l'égalité!*

In the image

There has been much debate over what it means to be created in the image of God. One approach can be ruled out immediately: there is no suggestion that we are physical representations of what God looks like. In Christ, God reveals himself to us in bodily form; by the Holy Spirit, God reveals himself to us as a spiritual being. He reaches down to our level of existence, communicating eternal mysteries and unfathomable depths of truth in ways we can understand. But the old man in the sky with a white beard is a figment of Western imagination and a wretched misrepresentation of the God of the Bible. It is in our essential being, not in our bodily existence, that we are made in the image of God.

Genesis provides us with an open-ended statement. Rather than tying down all the implications for us, we are invited to tease out different aspects of the divine image. Six strands can readily be identified:

1 *We are moral beings.* Everyone has a conscience and some awareness of right and wrong, however much moral standards vary between individuals and societies.
2 *We are rational beings.* Or at least we are capable of reason, as Jonathan Swift once observed with characteristic precision. Reason allows us to investigate life itself, analysing data and developing interpretative theorems.
3 *We are spiritual beings.* Our existence is more than material. We are instinctively religious, seeking meaning and purpose in life, offering

worship and prayer, and searching for transcendent realities beyond the mundanities of our daily routines.

4 *We are creative beings*. We take pleasure in appreciating beauty, whether in art or nature. No matter how limited our artistic talent, we find fulfilment in expressing our creativity, whether in painting or poetry, gardening or home decoration, clothing or jewellery. We don't want a lifestyle that is merely functional, instinctively making space for some kind of adornment and beauty.

5 *We are self-aware beings*. We are conscious not merely of our actions, but of our underlying motivations and other people's responses to us. We evaluate ourselves, and experience pleasure and pride, guilt and shame. And we are capable of personal development through self-assessment and target setting. We want to discover who we are and determine who we will become.

6 *We are relational beings*. Genesis 1:26 rather mysteriously uses the first person plural when God speaks – 'Let us'. From the perspective of the New Testament, this can be seen as an early indication that God is self-revealed in Trinity. Father, Son and Holy Spirit are three persons in one Godhead. For all eternity, God has enjoyed triune relationships of perfect love. Since we have been made in the image of God in community, human beings are made for community. We are not fully ourselves in isolation. The more we enjoy a network of loving and mutually supportive relationships, the more we can find ourselves and enjoy personal fulfilment. (That's why prolonged, solitary imprisonment is a punishment both cruel and inhumane.) The image of God in humankind is seen more fully when we are in positive relationships than in any isolated individual.

Men and women together

Men and women are made in the image of God together. That is, not only are men and women both made in the image of God, and not only are we made so equally, but the image of God finds fullest expression through men and women together. This should encourage us to cultivate a sense of partnership, both at work and at leisure. We give fullest expression to the image of God when working in harmony. That means we need to learn not merely how to put up with one another, but how to be enriched by our various contributions. In short, we have to make a shift from gender rivalry to gender complementarity, because that's the way God intended life to be enjoyed to the full. The image of God is made manifest in the interaction of men and women, and so we have the potential to bring out the best in one another, as we learn to work effectively in partnership. Men and women are better together.

Two more invaluable insights into male–female relationships are provided by Genesis 1–3. First, Eve is defined as Adam's 'suitable helper' (Gen. 2:18, 20). This begs the question as to what sort of helper did God decide to provide? Could this mean that Eve was created to be the junior assistant, the cleaner, cook and bottle washer, the general dogsbody serving the master of the house? Or, on the contrary, could it imply that the helper is always stronger than the helped, like a parent who comes to assist a young child incapable of completing a task on his or her own? The meaning of the phrase becomes clear by looking further into the Old Testament.

The word 'helper' is occasionally used to describe military aid (Isa. 30:5; Hos. 13:9) – in Hollywood terms, the helper is like the cavalry riding over the hill. The most common Old Testament usage describes divine assistance – God is my helper (e.g. Gen. 4:1; Exod. 4:15; Deut. 33:7, 29; Ps. 54:4). The idea that God would function as our junior partner is quite absurd, and so the use of this same word to describe the woman's role necessarily elevates her beyond any thought of subordination.

We find further clarification in the use of the word 'suitable' to describe this particular kind of 'helper'. The Hebrew phrase is not found again in the Old Testament and literally translates as 'like opposite', which means a matching partner. This excludes any notion of an unequal partnership where one or the other is dominant. Women and men are therefore invited to see one another as matching partners. The phrase 'suitable helper' is intended to inspire us to enter into mutuality, with two-way respect, support, benefit and appreciation. We can enjoy our complementarity in creative partnership, not just in marriage, but in every aspect of life.

In the next chapter of Genesis a new factor enters the equation: '. . . your husband, and he will rule over you' (Gen. 3:16). The context for this statement is not God's creation ordinances (Gen. 1–2), nor the divinely appointed basis for marriage (Gen.

2:24–5). On the contrary, the first time we encounter husbands ruling over their wives is in one of God's judgement speeches after the Fall. In short, male chauvinism, gender inequality, wife beating, sexual abuse and rape – that is, male domination in all its forms, whether socially acceptable or totally repugnant – are a result of the Fall and a sign of sin. God's appointed best for men and women is complementarity and mutual respect. It is because of our sinfulness that relationships between men and women degenerate so readily into hierarchy and mutual antipathy.

The remarkable affirmation in Genesis 1–3 of human equality, compatibility and complementarity in God's creation purposes has many important and practical implications:

1 *Disciples of Christ should avoid gender 'put-downs'*. For example, 'Women drivers' or 'I wouldn't expect any better from a man'.
2 *We should avoid gender stereotyping*. For example, 'All women are intuitive' or 'No women make good engineers'.
3 *We should take a stand against all forms of sexual discrimination and harassment*. This applies to the workplace, and to every other part of life, including church.
4 *We should avoid male-centred language that distracts from our mutual partnership as men and women*. For example, 'humankind' is better than 'mankind', 'servants of God' is preferable to 'men of God', 'children of God' is more inclusive than 'sons of God'.
5 *We need to cultivate a climate of mutual appreciation, where we are keen to learn from one another*. For example, I have sat on some national committees where the women are very quiet during the discussion. Sometimes this is because the mode of discourse is very male- centred, and we need to learn a new adaptability, new ways of structuring the meeting, in order to bring out the best in everyone.

We have a wonderful opportunity to explore the positive implications of God's gift in creation. Men and women together are made in the image of the triune God. And so we can learn to affirm and enjoy our equality, our complementarity and our partnership. According to Genesis 1–3, men and women are better together. In a world where gender roles are provoking much debate, uncertainty and conflict, Christian disciples have a wonderful opportunity to demonstrate a better way. We can express to our mutual benefit the fullness of the image of God as women and men learn to live in the harmony the Creator intended.

Beyond racism

When I was a teenager, most of the jokes we told at secondary school were about three kinds of people: women, Jews and Afro-Caribbeans. The schoolboy humour established a clear hierarchy in society: white males were at the top, and it was OK to sneer at women, be anti–Semitic, and to treat black people as second-class citizens. What's more, it was standard practice in those days to use the word 'spastic' as an insult.

Hostility towards minority groups seems endemic. In July 1999 a storm of controversy surrounded a hospital in Sheffield when it was revealed that an organ donor had specified that their body parts could only be given to a white patient. Even when racial and sexual discrimination have been made illegal, the underlying prejudices of institutional racism and sexism run deep within us.

Genesis 1 requires us to recognise that the image of God is intrinsic to every single human being. It has nothing to do with our gender, our ethnic origin, our accomplishments, our wealth, our social status, our age or whether we suffer from any kind of disability. Every single human being is worthy of respect, and there is a sanctity to every human life. We don't achieve the image of God through our own achievements; it is ours by birthright. To be human is to be made in God's image, however much others may admire or revile us.

This places a fourfold responsibility upon any Christian who is seeking to pursue whole-life discipleship:

1 We must make every effort to eradicate all kinds of sexism, racism, ageism, and negative attitudes towards the disabled from our own behaviour and thinking.
2 We must make every effort to eradicate all expressions of these prejudices from our church.
3 We must promote the eradication of all such prejudices from our work and leisure environments.

4 Above all, we need to go far beyond the mere eradication of denigratory attitudes and learn to give positive affirmation and appreciation to every human being, since all of us, without exception, are made in the image of God.

Chapter 4

Marriage – Made in Heaven?

TWO MEDIA STUNTS early in 1999 captured the news headlines. A radio station organised a marriage where the couple were hand-picked by a team of counsellors. The radio station organised the counselling, the marriage and a luxurious honeymoon. There was only one catch: the couple had not actually met until a couple of minutes before the wedding ceremony. It was like a turbo-charged version of TV's *Blind Date*. But now you stood to win a partner for life. There was not the slightest possibility that the couple could seriously mean the vows they declared when they barely knew one another's names. Not long after their return home, their break-up was announced.

A few weeks later a magazine sank to new depths of bad taste when they announced a competition where the first prize was a divorce – all expenses paid up to £500. All you had to do was write in and explain why it was impossible to live with your partner any longer. Such sensation-seeking makes a mockery of marriage. It also trivialises the immense pain that surrounds marriage break-down. The magazine was inviting their audience to adopt an impulsive, jokey and casual attitude towards one of the most traumatic decisions anyone can face.

The prizewinners in this bizarre pair of competitions became willing but foolish victims of a heartless marketing strategy. For the sake of five minutes of fame they were risking the long-term emotional well-being of themselves and those close to them. Only in a society obsessed with superficiality and the fast buck could marriage and divorce be considered legitimate prizes in a competition. Here was compelling new evidence of a world that is fast losing any grasp of the foundation of loving commitment and mutual respect upon which every healthy marriage is built.

Marriage is changing fast; that much is clear to everyone. More couples are divorcing and more are choosing to live together, either before they get married or without getting married at all. More children are being born outside of marriage, and the old stigma of illegitimacy seems to have evaporated. Before we consider the Bible's teaching on marriage, we need to explore some of the key factors in the changing face of marriage. I'm not wishing to suggest that all these factors are necessarily destructive, although some undeniably are. But if we are to understand the face of marriage in this generation, we need to recognise how our experience and expectations of marriage are becoming significantly different from previous eras.

The breakdown of fixed roles

When my grandparents got married, they knew exactly what they expected of one another. He would be the breadwinner and the disciplinarian; she would be the home-maker and the nurturer of their children. These roles were more or less universal: when their friends married, they all shared the same expectations of the roles of husbands and wives. The same job descriptions applied in almost every household.

The division of responsibilities on the first day of marriage remained more or less constant until such a time as ill health enforced adjustments. It was not only marriage that was for life, but there was also a permanent, standardised job description for husbands and wives. Today the roles are no longer standardised: who does what will vary from home to home. Nor are the roles permanent: in different seasons of life, modern marriages are more likely to experience an ebb and flow of responsibilities.

In the 1950s, it was still standard practice for a man to hand over the weekly housekeeping money. Today, men and women will usually have equal access to a joint bank account to which they both contribute their earnings. No serious attempt to strengthen twenty-first-century marriages can attempt to resurrect the style of marriage of a past generation. Housekeeping and slippers by the fire, the 'little woman at home', the fixed roles of breadwinner and home-maker, that era is dead and buried. And, many of us would say, a good thing too!

Today we have unprecedented opportunities to explore personal development in the context of marriage. The absence of fixed roles means liberation and new space for personal expression, as we learn to customise marriage in a way that suits us best as a couple at this particular stage of our lives. But this new freedom also makes more important than ever before the need to communicate and listen well, so that we really learn to hear and understand one another's aspirations. Otherwise, the potential for a married couple to experience personal growth together is likely to be shipwrecked by conflicting expectations and escalating misunderstanding. The skills of negotiation, flexible attitudes and giving priority to the other's needs are crucial. There is simply no place for any attempts by one-half of a couple to impose by diktat the inflexible and standardised roles of yesteryear.

Two-career couples

The old assumption was that women would normally sacrifice any thought of a career after a couple got married. Today, many couples take it for granted that both have an opportunity, or even an entitlement, to fulfil their potential in the workplace. For some, this is not so much an opportunity as a practical necessity. The cost of housing in some parts of the country is so prohibitive that two incomes are required simply to finance a mortgage. More money naturally brings hazards as well as opportunities. The availability of easy credit for two-income families has led some into the trap of excessive personal debt. This inevitably puts immense strain upon a relationship, even if both parties have been equally wanton with the credit cards.

When husband and wife are both working outside the home, an entirely new dynamic is introduced to the marriage relationship. In the traditional marriage, a man would come in and collapse by the fire or television, while his wife waited upon him, handing him his slippers and his evening meal. But in the modern marriage, *both* come home tired; thus there is no longer one breadwinner who can claim the right to slump in an armchair while the partner is busy in the kitchen. It may make sense for one partner to do most of the cooking, but only if the other takes responsibility for their fair share of regular household chores.

New dilemmas also arise when two-career couples face the implications of promotion and moving house. In the traditional marriage, a typical husband may not even have thought to consult his wife, but simply informed her of the need to move house, after accepting promotion. The wife's chief contribution to the decision was to congratulate her husband upon his success. In the modern marriage, both careers are implicated in any prospect of moving house. One partner's promotion may mean less time to contribute to the upkeep of the home, and their partner's career may even be compromised as a result of their advancement. Or perhaps both will enjoy rapid promotion, and the escalating demands of the workplace mean that the remnants of time left for one another become ever more threadbare. Success at work can make a failure of our home lives.

The care of children can become a difficult juggling act when there are two careers to consider. In the traditional marriage, a brood of children were expected to begin to arrive in the early years of wedlock, and they were a wife's expected focus of attention for the next quarter of a century. Today there are new expectations. An increasing number of couples have chosen to delay starting a family, partly in order to become fully established in their careers. The trouble is that there is never a convenient time to have children. And having them is only the start of many years of dependency. It is no longer obvious to every couple that the wife's work is automatically the career more easily interrupted in order to provide child-care during the early years. While the number of men who choose to stay at home is still a tiny minority, more of them can now be seen, hovering uncertainly at the edge of parent-toddler groups. Whichever partner stays at home for the sake of nurturing young children, there is a risk that an underlying resentment may emerge, either towards the partner or the children, if their career never seems to recover from the months or years spent away from the workplace.

Further complications are likely to arise when parenthood is deferred. The relentless ticking of the biological clock can bring escalating tensions. And while a wealthy couple in their early forties may lavish goodies upon their new baby, who sometimes begins to look like their latest lifestyle acquisition, when they are nearing their sixtieth birthdays their children will only just be getting into the swing of adolescence. At forty, a sixteen-year-old child can be exhausting; at sixty, it may all become too much. And the later we have children, the less time we will have to enjoy grandchildren and contribute our love and affection to their upbringing.

The two-career couple can also bring to the surface male insecurities. Traditional, cultural expectations remain deeply ingrained in the human spirit. Many younger men are in principle very committed to their wife's freedom to pursue her own career. But if she becomes more successful, and starts earning a higher income, some husbands can become very threatened. The cultural tradition that the husband is 'meant to be the breadwinner' can make some men feel insecure, or even a complete failure. If such feelings are not acknowledged and dealt with in a healthy and open way, they can result in an underlying anger, a lack of confidence and passivity, and even emotional or sexual dysfunction.

Life expectancy

The longer we live, the longer we are faced with enjoying or enduring the same marriage partner. In the days before modern medicine, many women died in pregnancy and childbirth, and their husbands would usually remarry. A long-lived man could reasonably anticipate several wives in his lifetime. At the same time, women who survived the childbearing years were quite likely to lose their husband at a time of life that we would now call early middle age. Marriage for life certainly seems to have been taken more seriously in previous generations: but the duration of this particular kind of life sentence, for better or worse, was in practice often relatively short. For those who enjoy a normal life-span in the West today, marriage at twenty that lasts a lifetime means about sixty years, or three-quarters of life, spent in a single relationship. The possibility of being married for much longer than in previous generations means greater opportunities and demands within the marriage: *opportunities*, because a successful marriage can continue to thrive and develop; *demands*, because there is more time for the marriage to go stale and for a couple to become thoroughly bored with each other, or even hostile towards one another.

Divorce expectancy

The marriage vows still speak of 'till death do us part', but divorce has become increasingly normal. What once was frowned upon, and was then considered a misfortune, has now become so familiar as to come as no surprise. The expectation that a high percentage of marriages will fail, coupled with divorce laws that have made it ever more easy to terminate a marriage, have resulted in a new attitude to marriage breakdown. In an age of instant answers, when difficulties arise in a marriage it seems easier to give up than to try to work through the problems. I have met couples who have walked away from their marriage as a result of a difficulty or problem that their parents or grandparents would have considered trivial. A determined attitude that we can work it out has been replaced by short-termism – if there's no quick fix, let's call it a day and try again with someone else. 'Stickability' has given way to disposable relationships. Some trade in their marriages as casually as others trade in a secondhand car. One solicitor recently observed on television that 'unreasonable behaviour' as a basis for divorce in English law means that anyone who wants a divorce can obtain it easily, since 'everyone has been unreasonable within a fortnight of getting married'. It is doubtful that this was the actual intention of the politicians who originally framed this piece of legislation.

The children of divorced parents very often bring the experience of breakdown in their parents' relationship to their own marriages. While some show an increasing reluctance to risk marriage at all, others have our society's prevailing attitude towards marriage as an increasingly short-term relationship, greatly reinforced by their own painful experiences. While Hollywood stars may have set the trend for multiple marriages as a result of divorce, those whose immediate family have all been divorced can bring an almost fatalistic attitude to their own marriage. 'I'm the only one in my family not to have been divorced,' Dave explained to me, 'and so I'm bracing myself for the marriage breakdown that now seems almost guaranteed.' There were no great problems in Dave's marriage at the time, but the expectancy of divorce was sapping his confidence in his ability to sustain a long-term, loving relationship.

Sex without consequences

Perhaps the greatest discouragement to casual sex in previous generations was the threat of an unwanted pregnancy. The contraceptive revolution has dramatically severed sexual activity from the prospect of parenthood. Since the availability of the contraceptive pill, couples have been able to plan their family with unprecedented precision. This has inevitably demoted childbearing as a purpose of marriage. In previous eras, fertile couples could confidently expect the rapid onset of parenthood once they became sexually active. Today, a couple can enjoy sexual relations as an expression of an intimate relationship without any thought that a visit to Mothercare is likely to be imminent.

Sex without conception has been very freeing for many married couples, greatly enriching the sexual side of their relationship. But it has also made both living together and casual sex more readily available. The close link between sexual activity and marriage has therefore been severed. Today, over 90 per cent of couples have slept together before marriage. Virginity is widely considered an embarrassing problem that needs solving urgently in teenage years, rather than a privilege to be preserved for sharing with one's marriage partner.

This new attitude to sex alters our society's approach to marriage. More people are entering marriage having already experienced several sexual partners. The connection between sexual relations and the marriage bond has been weakened dramatically. Without the threat of pregnancy, sex is being entered into casually, impulsively and without any notion of its consequences. A sexual radical of the 1960s summed up this new attitude by claiming that having sex with someone had no more significance than shaking their hand. Hollywood usually glamorises casual sex and yet occasionally explores its hazardous pitfalls. In the film *Fatal Attraction*, a brief sexual encounter was shown to have unpredictable and disastrous consequences, establishing a continuing bond between people, no matter how casual their original coupling.

In global terms, the majority of Aids sufferers are heterosexual. However, in the West the threatened explosion of the virus beyond the homosexual community has never happened. As a result, the Aids pandemic seems not to have raised serious questions about casual, unprotected sex or a lasting change in sexual attitudes in the heterosexual community. The alarm bells about unsafe sex have been muffled and the prevailing assumption is to consider sex a pleasurable activity of the present moment, instantly gratifying and without any lasting consequences, neither emotional nor physical, and certainly not, with due precautions, parental. Above all, this attitude towards unprotected sex remains common among younger generations, who tend to approach life with a built-in assumption of their own immortality.

Living together

For increasing numbers, there is little to choose between living together and getting married. Some want to get married to ink over a relationship in which they have shared bed and home for several years. Others speak of marriage largely in terms of the wedding day. Their aspirations seem to centre on the dress and the presents, the reception and the photos.

When living together first became more common, some described it as a 'trial marriage'. The theory was that you made sure you were compatible, emotionally and sexually, before entering into the marriage bond, which would then be stronger as a result of these careful preparations. In practice, the statistics now reveal that living together actually has the opposite impact, undermining a relationship's durability. When couples have been living together before marriage, the marriage bond is less likely to last.

The underlying issue seems to be commitment. By definition, a couple who are living together reserve the right to call the relationship off at any time. Living together is a provisional relationship, no matter whether the couple's intentions are serious and long-term or casual and temporary. This experience of a relationship that could have a limited 'shelf life' tends to be carried over into any subsequent marriage. If you know that the relationship could end at any time, it is only sensible to protect a clear sense of your separate identity, distinct from your experience as a couple. It's not just a matter of making sure you keep your CD collection intact. You are obliged to defend your inner self from a full and unreserved sense of oneness with your partner for the simple reason that your relationship, no matter how loving, has a high risk of built-in obsolescence.

Living together has a profoundly corrosive influence upon any understanding of marriage as a covenant relationship. In a covenant, you make a binding commitment to your partner. It is a decision of the will and the dedication of a lifetime. The traditional, Christian marriage vows do not dwell on how we feel about one another. This is not because feelings are unimportant, but because they are not enough on their own to secure a lasting relationship. We do not pledge ourselves to one another until someone better comes along, nor for as long as we feel like it. We make a solemn vow to which we commit ourselves for life. These four attitudes – living together, living impulsively, living selfishly and living according to our feelings – have come together at the end of the twentieth century to create an outlook that finds lifelong vows to be an alien or even incomprehensible basis for a loving and lasting relationship. Because these attitudes have become so prevalent in our society, there is now a desperately short supply of love that lasts.

Hollywood fantasies

Incalculable damage has been done to some people's expectations of marriage in general, and sex in particular, as a result of Hollywood. 'Body doubles' for the big name stars perform with gymnastic athleticism in sex that is always successful, spectacular, fulfilling and orgasmic. Such footage creates expectations that will never be met in the average bedroom. Magazines fuel this obsession with 'having sex' rather than 'making love'. Tender feelings are usurped by an over-intense quest for sexual achievement and performance. The result of this obsession with sexual superficiality is at least bruised egos; at worst, broken hearts and damaged lives.

Increasing demands

Most people today live with very limited experience of an extended family. Children go away to college, move somewhere else for their first job, and by then their parents have often moved house too. With our frequent use of removal vans, we have become the nomadic generations of the technological age. Parents and grandparents rarely live within walking distance. This loss of extended family also means the loss of rootedness in any particular community. Once we have moved house a couple of times, and so have our childhood friends, many of us have little remaining experience of a place where we instinctively and always belong. Like snails, our home is taken with us, and there is no particular town or village that still feels like home.

Not everyone experiences quite this degree of uprootedness, but the continuing breakdown of community means that more and more is demanded of our marriage relationships. A long-term trend in beer drinking illustrates our increasing focus upon the home: people are buying less beer in pubs, where it is drunk on the premises, and more beer from off-licences and supermarkets, drinking in the privacy of our own homes. What uprootedness means, especially for those who don't know their neighbours, is that our marriage partner is both our lover and our best friend. With the absence of a wider framework of relationships, we lean more heavily upon one another than in previous generations.

For some couples, this brings great joy, because they would naturally be one another's best friend in any kind of society. For others, the demands are too great, and without the support structures of a settled community and a wide circle of friends, the emotional and social strains placed upon the marriage become too much to bear. With no other close and continuing relationships, the marriage partner cannot always take the strain. This problem of increasing emotional and social demands is illustrated by the times of year when the demand for marriage counselling is highest. Just after Christmas and the summer holidays, couples in deteriorating relationships find unbearable the experience of spending more time than usual in one another's company.

Two or three generations ago, most couples had to devote a great deal of their energy to survival: working hard simply to earn a living and raise the children left little time or opportunity for higher aspirations. Today, the vast majority of couples in the West are no longer struggling to put food on the table, or living from hand to mouth. As a result, higher aspirations develop not only for what we want from life, but also for what we expect from our marriage partner. We naturally begin to emphasise quality of life, our continuing development as individuals, and the fulfilment of our potential. In previous generations, it was enough to bring home a weekly wage, to keep the house clean, and ensure the children were fed. But now, we expect our marriage partner to give us room to grow with the passing of years. If they become too settled, too inflexible, we may even begin to resent them, feeling that they are holding us back from our full potential. It is no longer enough for marriage to help us cope with life's rigours, we also expect that our marriage should bring us ever-increasing personal fulfilment.

Less support, greater expectations

We live in a society that does little or nothing to support or promote healthy and successful marriages. Even the tax system in Britain has a built-in bias against marriage, taxing married couples more heavily than those who live together. That is surely an extraordinary example of perverse social engineering! The resources our culture provides to help couples to sustain and enjoy a good marriage seem to be steadily eroding. At the same time, the demands and expectations we place upon our marriages are steadily increasing. This is a dangerous cocktail: increased demands combined with reduced resources can only lead to a sense of pressure and fragility.

Many experience disappointment or frustration in their marriage; some fear that their marriage is inevitably brittle and at risk; others become more or less resigned to the likely collapse of their marriage as an almost unavoidable destiny in this generation. We need to face squarely the destructive expectations and contradictory pressures to which all too many modern marriages have succumbed. If our society's experience of marriage is to become more successful and rewarding, we need to explore creatively how to turn today's pressures into new opportunities for relationships that can thrive, not merely survive. In the timeless wisdom of the Bible we discover not a rigid blueprint relevant only in the ancient world, but a remarkably adaptable and creative set of values and insights that are still capable of empowering marriages to flourish once again in the twenty-first century.

God's gift

We have explored at length the pressures upon modern marriages for a very simple reason. Christian disciples do not get married in a religious cocoon, totally isolated from the values and expectations of their society. We may be relatively unscathed by some of these escalating pressures; but we live out our discipleship in a particular social context, and so our marriages will inevitably share in many of the pressures and opportunities we have identified. It's no use an older Christian calling us back to the good old days of the fixed roles of a 1950s marriage. The Word of God may last for ever, but yesterday's world has gone. Whole-life discipleship means applying timeless biblical principles to the marriages of the world of today and tomorrow, not trying to raise yesterday from the dead.

In Genesis 2, marriage is presented not merely as a human institution but as God's gift in creation. It is the foundational building block of human society, the basis of stability and the nucleus of civilisation. The Church has lapsed into two extreme attitudes towards marriage. In the medieval era, marriage was the option of second-class Christians. To be truly spiritual required singleness and celibacy. Sexual activity and spiritual purity were considered incompatible. This prejudice is without foundation in the New Testament. In the modern era, many Protestant churches have ended up at the opposite extreme, conveying the impression that marriage is necessarily superior to singleness. There are churches that would never contemplate a single minister or elder – which would, of course, rule out Jesus as well as many other early Christian leaders. This prejudice is equally without biblical justification.

So why should we consider marriage within the context of whole-life discipleship? Isn't this a subject solely of concern to those who are married or about to be married? Because marriage is presented in Genesis as a creation ordinance, we all need to understand the biblical teaching that establishes the key ingredients for a healthy marriage. Exploring this teaching is likely to help our own home life if we are married, but can also be advantageous for the marriages of our friends and colleagues. What's more, some aspects of this teaching are also profoundly important for single people to attain full adult maturity and inner security.

When people think about getting married in Britain today, they are likely to picture the bridal gown and everyone dressed smartly, the photos and the guests, the reception and the presents, the cake and the wedding breakfast. But all of these things are ultimately optional extras. They happen to be the way a particular society has celebrated weddings, but they have little to do with the essence of marriage according to God's creation purposes. Genesis 2:24 provides three universal principles. The more we are able to understand and apply them, the more healthy and rewarding our marriages are likely to become.

Leaving

In the words of Genesis, a man must leave his father and mother. The wedding day is a time of sadness as well as joy for the couple's parents, because there is a very real sense in which they are losing a child. From this day forward there will be a new primary relationship for the newly married couple. They both need to learn how to put their marriage partner before their parents. In order to tie the knot, we must cut the apron strings.

This is symbolised in traditional British weddings by the giving away of the bride. This reflects the patriarchal character of British society. The woman is handed over from the father to the husband, entering the jurisdiction of a new overlord. This is given lasting expression by the woman taking her husband's surname. But notice the radicalism of Genesis, where it is emphasised that the *man* will leave his father and mother. In Western society it has sometimes seemed that the woman leaves her family in order to join her husband's. In Genesis, the fact that the man leaves his family is not meant to imply the opposite of our traditions – namely, that the man joins the woman's family. Rather, it speaks of a mutual leaving of the parental homes and the old family identities, in order to establish a new life together.

The traditional practice of giving away the bride has often been understood to have unambiguously patriarchal overtones. But it could easily be reinterpreted in a more profound and fully biblical way. Instead of the bride's father standing on his own and handing over the woman to her future husband, all the parents could stand and together acknowledge that they are presenting the couple to be married. In this way, the parents are accepting the necessary price of marriage: for the couple to enter fully into their new union together, the parents must relinquish any claim to come first in their children's lives.

    — *Who gives this man and woman to be married?*
    — *We do!*

My own conviction is that this would add a very helpful emphasis to the wedding service. Nonetheless, the main responsibility for leaving lies with the couple who are getting married. Their parents can help by willingly letting them go, rather than trying to impose inappropriate demands. But the couple must make decisive choices for themselves. What's more, it is highly unlikely that leaving could ever be completed at the wedding ceremony. Marriage is both an event and a new way of life into which we learn to grow. This means that leaving is given a symbolic expression during the wedding service, but it is also a journey that the newly married couple must learn to walk together. Moreover, leaving is not only a crucial foundation for a healthy marriage, it is just as important for the single person who wishes to establish full independence as a mature, self-realised adult.

Leaving requires that we learn to find our own way as a couple, instead of imposing 'my family's way'. Because we are used to our parents' way of doing things, it is very likely that we will take some aspects of home life for granted, assuming that the customs we are used to are standard practice everywhere. In many details of life a couple will need to discover their own way together: where to squeeze the toothpaste tube and where to leave it after use; whether to shut doors or leave them open when leaving a room; whether washing-up is best done directly after a meal or delayed until after a cup of coffee.

Failure to leave our parents can lead to misunderstandings or even prove disastrous. Claire and I counselled one couple who were having problems managing their money. In Rick's family, his mother had always paid the bills. In Sue's, it was her father's responsibility. Rick thought bills were women's work. Sue thought bills should be left to men. They didn't discuss their different expectations. They both assumed that their own parents' way of doing things simply had to be right. Whenever a bill came through the door, they both ignored it. When a red bill arrived, whoever paid it did so grudgingly, blaming their partner for failing to comply with their unspoken expectations. Only by abandoning their parents' methods and agreeing their own approach could sanity be restored to their financial affairs!

One acid test of whether we have really left our parents is what happens when they visit our home. Does the mother or mother-in-law take over in the kitchen? Cath went into a frenzy for a week before Mark's mother visited. We found her bleaching all the cups. 'Cath, what are you doing?' Claire asked. 'Oh,' she exclaimed, pausing for the briefest moment, 'Mark's mother likes to inspect everything to make sure I'm looking after him properly.' The responsibility to deal with this overbearing attitude rested with Mark and his mother. Mark needed to stand up for his wife, and tell his mother as graciously as possible to back off. Mark's mother needed to let go and accept that she entered their home as a family guest, not as an environmental health inspector or an overbearing matriarch.

Peter had lunch with his mother every day. He'd always gone home for lunch before he got married, and without a thought the habit continued. His parents had divorced, and he felt responsible for his mother. He also enjoyed her company – no one had ever understood him quite as well as his mother. Stephanie didn't want to be possessive of her new husband, and she admired his concern for his mother, but she would have liked the two of them to have lunch together some days. Stephanie knew she was important to Peter, but she felt that she was very definitely second-best to his mother. Leaving our parents does not mean rejecting them, but we do need to show our partner, and our parents if necessary, that the marriage relationship comes first.

Parents need to help their children to leave. We can become over-protective when our children need to learn to do things for themselves. And we can become over-demanding when our children need space to develop their own lives. The principle of leaving is crucial for healthy marriage, which is why it is emphasised in Genesis 2. It is also profoundly important for adult singles, freeing them to develop their own identity fully and freely. Once we have learned to leave, things will never be the same. But we don't have to become distant. Those who have established a clear sense of leaving their parents are then in a position to develop an adult closeness with them: a different kind of loving for a new stage of life.

Being united

Genesis 2 explains that the second crucial factor for every healthy marriage is that we bond together. This does not mean a loss of our individual identity. It's no justification for one partner being overwhelmed or absorbed by the other. Rather it speaks of a new and lasting togetherness, a covenant relationship in which we dedicate ourselves to our partner's well-being.

On the wedding day, we express our new unity through the vows we share. This is given legal expression through signing a register and may be symbolised through an exchange of rings. But marriage is a living relationship and not just an event. In order to continue to be united, we have to keep working at our marriage.

Being united requires time together. This is often effortless in the early days of marriage, when young love carries us on a tide of enthusiasm. With the passing of years, developing careers can take up more and more of our time. And while some babies are no trouble at all, others make sure that their presence cannot go unnoticed for more than twenty minutes, day or night. As a result, many couples will go through a stage of marriage when they become increasingly busy and increasingly tired. In such seasons of life, it is all too easy to give up on quality time together. We then give one another the leftovers of our time and gradually drift apart.

Early romance gives way sooner or later to realism, as we see one another's strengths and limitations more clearly. At this point we can move in one of two directions. We can grow deeper into a clear-sighted love for one another, or we can grow further apart, resigned to disappointment with our partner and looking elsewhere for our fulfilment, whether at work or leisure or with someone else.

I have met couples who have slipped into an experience of parallel lives, existing in the same house but functioning as isolated individuals. Others fall into the trap of relating to one another only through their children. They may function well at the level of father and mother, but are neglecting to invest in their primary relationship as husband and wife. In my early days in pastoral ministry I came across two couples who were paying the price for neglecting their marriage while investing in their children. Jack's and Helen's children were in their late teens and early twenties, and the last was about to leave home. Pete's and Paula's youngest was about to go to school, giving Paula much more time for herself. In both cases, these couples recognised the need to spend more time together, but they were at a loss to know what to do. What disturbed me greatly was that both husbands asked me the same questions: 'I think it would be a good idea for us to spend more time together, but what do you suggest we do? And what do you think we could talk about?' The tragic reality of living parallel lives is that by the time many people wake up to the problem, their marriage is already in a massive relational deficit. To restore the marriage they will need to devote a great deal of time and effort to getting to know one another all over again.

Couples have to find their own, personal ways of spending quality time together. For some it may be a video and a curry. For others, a night at the opera and a restaurant meal. Some will be able to act on impulse, while others live with such a full diary that they will have no choice but to become organised and make time for one another in their schedules. What matters is not that we copy someone else's way of doing things, but that we choose togetherness – according to whatever pattern works for us as a couple.

Being united isn't just about time, it's also about understanding one another – and that means listening. Claire likes to debrief at the end of a busy day by talking everything through with me. But I like to leave the day behind by slumping in a chair, switching off, and not talking at all. Claire can get frustrated if she is talking away and the only response I am giving is a badly timed grunt of interest. From Claire's perspective, I'm not listening when she needs me to. From my perspective, Claire's debriefing is interrupting my time away from life's demands. These differences could turn into pointless friction and frustration. Like any other couple, we need to be honest with one another and work out a flexible compromise that gives both of us enough of what we need.

A recent questionnaire asked British couples how much time they liked to spend talking together in a personal way. Women said forty minutes; men said twelve. It gets worse: the women expected forty minutes a *day*, but the men thought they could cope with twelve minutes a *week*! Those familiar with the cartoon family the Simpsons would probably say that there is something of Homer Simpson in most men! Maybe men cannot scale the full heights of women's conversational expectations, but at least we have to learn how to meet them part way. There are different levels of conversation: passing a greeting; conveying factual information; expressing our opinions; revealing our feelings; a real heart-to-heart encounter. Quality time together requires us to make the effort to get down to the deeper levels of conversation. We have to learn – men especially – that it really is good to talk.

Learning to listen is about more than opening our ears. We have to learn to make the effort to understand what is really being said. I'm not suggesting that we should have to spend a lot of time decoding one another's hints. Hinting rather than speaking plainly is a style of conversation most marriages could do without. When someone gets into a habit of hinting, they can begin to resent their partner for not acting on the hint. If we want people not to misunderstand us, we owe it to them to express our views and desires clearly.

Even in a hint-free relationship, there are many times when our words convey more than their literal meaning. We may communicate tiredness or disappointment, vulnerability or confusion. When our partner really matters to us, we want to listen to them at depth and not just superficially. The more we listen to and understand our partner, the more we can respond to their needs even before they have found a way to put them into words.

Being united means an end to rivalry and resentment. We have no need to compete with one another, and the New Testament expressly tells us to keep no record of wrongs (1 Cor. 13:5). As soon as someone uses this kind of phrase in an argument – 'That's the fifth time this month . . .' – they have put themselves in the wrong. Over the years many of us build up a repertoire of ways to win an argument, but if our first priority is to be united with our partner, we should rule out many of those ways of speaking even before the words pass our lips. The language of accusation – 'You always . . .', 'You never . . .' – has little value to a couple who want to continually strengthen their oneness and build one another up with a free flow of appreciation and affection.

Some people are instinctive bullies, dominating their partner and forever imposing their imperious will. Others are manipulative, always ending up with getting their own way by more indirect means. Being united means putting our partner first, listening to their point of view, and refusing to dig in our heels in endless and automatic stubbornness. If we treat our marriage like a battlefield, we may end up fighting to the death.

Oneness doesn't mean cloning. Some couples express their oneness through very similar tastes. Other marriages thrive where the husband and wife have remarkably different preferences. Unity in love means that we are secure to grow as individuals, trying out new interests and developing our potential. So long as we experience an underlying oneness and know that we really do come first for one another, we can be free to enjoy the differences between us, rather than complaining. One practical expression of this freedom to be ourselves may be a separate bank account for personal treats. Not everyone will need this. But some people feel they would be depriving the family of funds if they spent money on themselves from a joint account. If so, why not agree a small sum to be set aside each month, knowing that your partner is entirely happy that this money is used 'just for you'.

Oneness in marriage must mean respect for one another. The person who is always putting down their partner, whether to others or to their face, has little grasp of the priority of becoming one. If we have many gifts to offer at church but we continually treat our partner badly at home, it would be better if we did not serve in public until we have got our act together in private. Whole-life discipleship requires those who are married to cherish, build up, appreciate and encourage their partner.

Sexual union

Love-making is God's wedding gift, not just for the newly married couple, but for life. Our sexuality is good and wholesome, according to the Bible. And the sexual dimension of human love is celebrated in the Song of Solomon. There are many myths surrounding sex, and whenever they get a grip on our lives they can undermine the marriage relationship.

1 Sex is not dirty

A sex-obsessed society would seem to have blown this myth out of the water, but there are still people with a lurking suspicion that the whole thing is unpleasant and unclean. These people can feel soiled by sex and soiled by their own sexual stirrings. In some cases, early experiences of abuse have left them traumatised. Others have picked up a disastrously negative attitude in reaction against the crude earthiness of late twentieth-century 'laddism'. Some are anti-sex because their parents were always embarrassed to talk about it, or because they have never heard sexuality affirmed as something that can be positive, rewarding and wholesome.

2 Sex is not just for men's pleasure

It has been said that men are like gas cookers, and women are like electric cookers. Both can get very hot, but they take a different amount of time to get there! Some men have never learned that love-making is mutual, and approach the act as something to satisfy their own sexual appetite, with little regard for their partner. Some women still have a 'lay back and think of the empire' mentality. The New Testament insists that the principle of mutuality and equality applies to our sexuality in marriage: 'The wife's body does not belong to her alone but also to her husband. In the same way, the husband's body does not belong to him alone but also to his wife. Do not deprive each other except by mutual consent and for a time . . .' (1 Cor. 7:4–5). There's no mistaking it, love-making is a privilege the married couple are meant to share on an equal basis.

3 Sex is not just for having children

The older wedding liturgies used to list having children as the number one purpose of marriage. This led to some Christians concluding that sex could only be a good thing if you were planning to conceive a child. Today, most of us have come to realise that love-making is a gift in itself, enriching for our marriage whether or not it produces children. While sexual union in the days before contraceptives was likely to lead quite regularly to conception, in Genesis it is the gift of being one flesh rather than any resultant children that is highlighted as the third vital ingredient for a healthy marriage. Sex is a good thing in itself as God's wedding gift to a married couple.

4 Sex is not just for young people

The first three hang-ups we have identified are now declining in our society, but new hang-ups are taking their place. When young people begin to experience their sexual awakening, it's often very difficult for them to imagine that their parents are still sexually active. As TV and Hollywood become more sexually explicit, the sexual activity is usually athletic, the actors young, beautiful and fit. Some Hollywood stars use body doubles for explicit scenes, not simply to preserve their own modesty, but in order to ensure that the body on the screen is without the slightest blemish. Movie sex is fantasy sex: it would not appeal to the audience if the bodies were older or were more typical of the general population. As a result, films can construct a distorted and narcissistic view of sexuality. According to the Bible, there is no automatic expiry date for the gift of sex in marriage.

5 Sex is not a casual act

With the widespread availability of contraception, we have experienced a revolution in attitudes to sex. A 1990 survey of British women in their twenties and thirties indicated that the majority expected to sleep with a boyfriend within the first few weeks of starting a relationship. 'Did you score last night?' is a question asked by many young men as they chalk up their fleeting conquests. Some tour companies have promoted singles holidays for those in their twenties as sun, sand, sangria and sex. The voracious pursuit of casual sexual conquests is the standard attitude among some young people today.

It's not the first time that a casual and consumerist attitude to sex has been common. Corinth was renowned in New Testament times as a city where sex was freely indulged and prostitution was widespread. Paul explained to the new converts in the Church he had recently established, that sleeping with someone involves more than our genitalia – we become 'one flesh' (1 Cor. 6:16). That is, the whole person is involved in the act of sexual union, in a way that is simply not true of other kinds of less intimate physical contact. We may never see the person again, but sexual intimacy has emotional and psychological consequences.

6 It's not just having sex

There are many different phrases in the English language to describe sexual union. 'Having sex', like most other common descriptions, concentrates on the physical act. It's a cold and consumerist phrase – it's about taking or achieving sexual conquest and fulfilment. That's why, when sex is approached selfishly, rape can occur between lovers, whether unmarried or married.

'Making love' is a so much more helpful phrase. The physical act of sexual union gives expression to and deepens our bonds of oneness in marriage. Animals have sex, people have a choice: we can choose just to have sex, or we can choose to make love. Genesis 2 ends with a striking phrase: 'naked and unashamed' (Gen. 2:25). This is not a slogan for some seedy backstreet strip-show. It's a description of the marital bedroom as God intended. Both physically and emotionally, the more we know that we are truly loved and accepted, the more secure we can feel so that we are able to let down our defences, relax, and enjoy one another.

Whole-life discipleship is not about disdaining sex, nor being too busy at work or church to have time for one another. True sexual fulfilment is found in the marriage relationship, where sexual union gives intimate and tender expression to a continuing experience of mutual support and appreciation. The more we feel loved, the more we are able to make love. The third dimension of God's foundations for marriage needs to find full and healthy expression in every Christian marriage.

Chapter 5

Science and Creativity

A FRIEND OF OURS remembers the introduction to the first university lecture she attended as a biology undergraduate. The lecturer, who was an ardent atheist, declared that if any of the students were Christians they would have to make a choice: either be a good Christian or a good scientist. This was a scandalous abuse of power because he was offering an entirely false choice. Senior members of that biology department were known to be Christians. Top scientists in every generation have been Christians. And when figures were compiled among university scientists it became apparent that the percentage of scientists who are Christians is actually higher than among the general population. Despite this evidence of people who are good scientists and faithful Christians, there is an underlying suspicion of conflict or contradiction. Some non-Christians will quickly come up with the excuse that 'science has disproved Christianity'. And some Christians without a scientific background, including some church leaders, adopt a wary, defensive, hostile or even dismissive attitude towards scientific study.

God's 'yes' to science

Genesis 1–3 declares God's 'yes' to science. There is a sequence of phased progress in God's work of creation, rather than everything happening at once, which is an invitation to us to explore development in the natural world. There is also a clear sense of orderliness. This means that creation can be classified and analysed. The orderliness of the cosmos also means that it is predictable and subject to cause and effect, rather than being arbitrary and whimsical. This means that the processes of cause and effect can be analysed, scientific theories can be extrapolated, and scientific laws can be established.

Adam was the first scientist. When he began naming the animals, that was the beginning of scientific classification. Solomon became internationally renowned for his wisdom, which included the study of botany, from cedar trees to rock plants, and biology, including animals, birds, reptiles and fish (1 Kings 4:33). He also compiled or composed 3,000 proverbs, which were understood to establish the laws of cause and effect in human existence, and the principles of right and prosperous living (1 Kings 4:32). This aspect of his learning can be understood as an early form of the social sciences. In short, Solomon is presented not merely in general terms as a great scholar king, but more particularly as ancient Israel's great scientist king.

We can trace several more ways in which Genesis 1 authenticates scientific investigation. Since we are made in the image of an orderly God, the human gift of reason is derived from the perfect rationality of the mind of God. When we discover how things work, from protons to the distant stars, we are discovering the divine craftsmanship and thinking God's thoughts after him. What's more, God created the material world and declared that it was very good. In other words, God is not just interested in spiritual and eternal things, but he invented matter, creating it directly and taking pleasure in his work. This is far from Greek notions of the gods. Some early Christians, influenced more by Greek philosophy than the Old Testament, developed theories in which God used inter-mediaries to create the material world since the divine would not want, or even could not possibly allow himself to be sullied by, anything beneath the very highest spiritual plane. The God of the Bible does not mind getting his hands dirty, as it were, taking pleasure in shaping the order and beauty of the material world.

Above all, Genesis 1 presents a God who is distinct from nature. There is one God, not a Constructor assembling existing elements, but a Creator who fashions out of nothing a cosmos that has a distinct and separate identity from himself. This is quite different from the pagan worlds of pantheism and animism. If God were in everything, or if particular gods dwelt in particular places, a spirit of the oak tree and a spirit of ants, we would dare not investigate the natural world. Paganism produces a deep fear that scientific investigation might trespass upon, intrude or disturb supernatural entities who in their anger would take revenge upon us. The Judaeo-Christian God's separation from nature is a charter for scientific enquiry.

The limits of science

Genesis legitimises science, but also sets some boundaries. First, science is made accountable. Ultimately this is to God, since we are custodians of creation on God's behalf. But science is also therefore accountable to a moral framework. We live in a world of increasing specialisation, and as a result there is an increasing pressure to leave ethical decisions to the specialists who, we are told, are the only ones capable of understanding all the complex issues. Of course we need to depend upon professional expertise, but there still needs to be a moral framework that sets appropriate boundaries to their work. This continues to be reflected in Britain by the invaluable inclusion of lay representatives upon British Medical Association and parliamentary ethics groups. As a society we continue to retain the conviction that we cannot surrender all responsibility for ethical decisions to a professional scientific elite.

Second, science must take account of fallenness. The tragic witness of history is that if a scientific innovation can be abused, it probably will be. For example, cloning can be looked at in several ways: (a) as an astonishing scientific breakthrough in the manipulation of the building blocks of life; (b) as a commercial gold mine for the companies that take control of the scientific processes; (c) as a licence for exploitation, with the twin dread possibilities of cloning a slave class, who are denied normal human rights, and the equally appalling prospect of cloning a thousand Hitlers, Pol Pots or Stalins.

Third, and above all, science is not theology, and must not be allowed to usurp the rightful issues of debate in a quite separate academic discipline. The proper questions of science are what, when and how. Theology focuses upon a quite different, although by no means incompatible, set of questions – that is, who and why. When scientists stray into theology and philosophy, they no longer speak with the authority they have earned in their own field of academic enquiry. For example, the theory of evolution addresses the question as to how species originate and develop. That is an entirely legitimate field of scientific enquiry. But evolutionism takes things a whole lot further and seeks to argue for a much wider conclusion that this rules out the possibility of God. But the scientific theory of evolution does not and cannot do any such thing. Whether we accept the theory of evolution unreservedly or find it unconvincing, the theory says much about the origin of species but nothing about the ultimate origin of life. The Darwinian theory leaves entirely unanswered the question whether there really is a Creator God who is the source of life and who set the cosmos in motion. And God has thus far not chosen to make himself subject to laboratory analysis.

Just as science is not theology, the reverse is also true. In Christian theology, Genesis 1 affirms that there is a Creator God. But the Bible is entirely agnostic about the mechanisms by which God originally brought creation into being and the mechanisms built into creation which enable its continued development. Genesis 1 offers no comment on the *how* of creation, preferring to concentrate upon the *who*. Therefore, just as the theory of evolution cannot disprove the doctrine of creation, the doctrine of creation can neither prove nor disprove the theory of evolution. Those Christians who claim that the doctrine of creation is necessarily anti-science are making a case just as weak as those atheists who claim that scientific theories are necessarily anti-creation. On the one hand, scientific investigation and theorems can neither prove nor disprove the existence of God. On the other hand, explorations into the *who* of creation, which is the focus of theology, cannot in themselves reveal the *how* of creation's origins and development.

So should the Christian who is also a scientist feel guilty or compromised, either in their faith or in their profession? Certainly not. The Christian who is a scientist can have their faith enriched and their explorations enhanced, as faith and reason work in harmony together. But let their dedication to exact measurement, acute analysis and precise and proven theories be matched by awe and wonder, delight and praise. Even so, if your interest in science is restricted to the occasional TV programme or magazine article, your fascination can turn to thankfulness before the Creator, the inventor of the totality of the cosmic design. The pursuit of science and the biblical doctrine of creation are thoroughly compatible. For the origin of all scientific discoveries, however revolutionary and unexpected, is found in the Eternal Mind of God.

Art and uncertainty

The arts have long had a bad press among many Christians. In calling churches back to the Bible, the Reformation tended to result in simpler buildings. Statues of Mary and the saints were avoided, or at least set in side chapels, and the empty cross became a more popular symbol among Protestants than an ornate crucifix. Un-adorned preaching replaced the colourful rituals of the mass as the central act of Christian worship.

At the time of the Restoration of the English monarchy, theatres were re-opened and quickly won a reputation as bawdy houses and places of ill-repute. The medieval tradition of mystery plays – community re-enactments of the great Bible stories – saw drama used in distinctively Christian ways. But from the time of the Restoration, many Christians became instinctively suspicious of all drama. Later it was the same with novels, which were frequently denounced as studies in immorality. One of the greatest novels ever, Gustave Flaubert's *Madame Bovary*, faced fierce opposition from churchmen who failed to understand its artistry and wanted it banned from publication.

Such attitudes do not die easily. In the 1980s I read of an American opera singer who was converted. As a result, she explained that she would not perform any role that involved immorality. If you know even a little about the operatic repertoire, you will know that this conviction would not leave her with many bookings at all. After the British actor, James Fox, decided to return to acting as a committed Christian, I became his publisher. Some Christians were so prohibitive in what they thought was appropriate subject material for a Christian actor that they would only have been happy if James had restricted himself to sentimental drama for children. One swear word, however mild, no matter what justification in the life of the character he was playing, was enough to convince them that he had become morally and spiritually bankrupt.

The general tendency among some Christians has been to assume that art needs to be justified. Some are happy with art so long as it is morally improving in a direct and unambiguous way. Others accept drama so long as it has an 'in-your-face' evangelistic thrust: but, of course, drama immediately loses its artistic integrity if it becomes manipulative and propagandist. When I was at theological college I took a leading role in a Tom Stoppard play – *The Real Inspector Hound.* It's typical Stoppard, much wit, much contrivance, with searching questions about human existence surfacing, however obliquely, from time to time. My college principal was a good and godly man, but he made it clear that he could not understand why we wanted to perform such a play. Sadly, the alternatives he suggested were tired, old moralistic productions by second-rate dramatists, well past their perform-by date.

In my publishing days I went each year to the annual conference of the American Christian publishers and booksellers. A major part of the sales in most bookstores was the 'holy hardware'. You could buy a welcome mat for your home imprinted with a Christian slogan, christianised Chinese fortune cookies with Bible verses inside, and every imaginable trinket. Protestants and Catholics have vied with one another in the bad taste stakes of religious kitsch. Some of the worst souvenirs I have ever seen were in Assisi. St Francis was a man dedicated to simplicity and deeply appreciative of the infinite beauties of creation. Lining the main street up to the great church built in his memory are innumerable shops filled with the most appalling garbage: nothing is too tacky, it seems, for the devout but undiscriminating tourist market. Crudely mass-produced statues, clumsily painted in garish colours, are, at least for me, a positive disincentive to explore Christian spirituality. They seem to indicate that to become a Christian you have to abandon all sense of taste.

Another common hang-up among Christians can be seen in the many posters of sublime scenery which are then adorned with a Bible verse. I'm not suggesting that the two kinds of communication are incompatible. Of course not. A well-chosen verse can help us to appreciate natural beauty more deeply. My hesitation is that some Christians have become so word-centred that they seem incapable of appreciating a photograph or a painting of the natural world unless a Bible verse is attached. Some painters evidently consider their work to be incomplete until an appropriate scripture has been inscribed over their brushwork. It's not fully Christian, they seem to feel, unless dependence on the Bible is made explicit. If Bible verses really were the proof-test of genuinely Christian art, then the Creator has missed the mark. Sacred texts are not built into the DNA of trees, so that every trunk has a Bible verse inscribed in its bark. God has obviously decided that natural beauty can speak for itself. Here is the sum of the problem: Christians have often wanted art to be propagandist, harnessed explicitly to the Christian cause. But God the Creator has other ideas. His artistry is art for art's sake, needing no justification beyond its own beauty, exquisite, breathtaking and wonderfully varied.

Art in the Old Testament

Because we are familiar with the writings of the ancient Israelites, we may have the superficial impression that they had little time for the other arts. Among the prophets, we find an appreciation of various art forms. Some were great storytellers. By the power of narrative, Nathan convicted David of his sin against Uriah the Hittite (2 Sam. 12). 'David burned with anger against the man [in Nathan's story] and said to Nathan, "As surely as the LORD lives, the man who did this deserves to die" ' (2 Sam. 12:5–7).

Some of the prophets were great poets, supremely Isaiah, in particular in the great lyrical poems of new beginnings such as chapter 40 and the songs of the suffering servant. Others gave public performances to convey their message, whether in mime or a short sketch with words. For example, as well as acting out the prospect of exile in many curious and striking ways, Ezekiel enacted the siege of Jerusalem as if he were a general preparing a strategy for war:

Now, son of man, take a clay tablet, put it in front of you and draw the city of Jerusalem on it. Then lay siege to it: Erect siege works against it, build a ramp up to it, set up camps against it and put battering-rams around it. Then take an iron pan, place it as an iron wall between you and the city and turn your face towards it. It will be under siege, and you shall besiege it. This will be a sign to the house of Israel. (Ezek. 4:1–3)

Jeremiah smashed a pot in a public place in order to give startling and unforgettable expression to the imminent judgement of God: 'Then break the jar while those who go with you are watching, and say to them, "This is what the LORD Almighty says: I will smash this nation and this city just as this potter's jar is smashed and cannot be repaired. They will bury the dead in Topheth until there is no more room" ' (Jer. 19:10–11). Such a dramatic moment certainly provoked an immediate reaction. The chief officer of the temple had him beaten up and locked in the public stocks overnight.

The psalms place great emphasis upon the arts. Although the Ten Commandments had excluded pictorial representations of God, the Jews made much of poetry and music. Many of the psalms express worship with great lyrical beauty. And the range of subject matter is rich, from thankful retelling of the broad sweep of national history to painful pleading with God in times of personal crisis, from celebrating the beauty of creation to meditating on the splendours of the law of the Lord. Here is no one-track, single-style, narrow expression of worship in words. Long deliberations are set alongside simple songs; the disclosure of personal anguish alongside the enthusiastic hymns of great national festivals.

The poetic richness of the psalms is matched by their breadth of use. Some psalms express such intense personal emotion, they can only find full expression when someone in extreme circumstances makes them their individual prayers. Some are poems for public events such as a coronation or a public procession to the temple, with the unmistakable sense of ceremonial accompanying a major event in national religious life. All of life is found in the psalms.

The ancient Jews were also keen on a wide range of musical instruments. The beauty of the poetry was enhanced by rich and harmonious sounds: 'Praise him with the sounding of the trumpet, praise him with the harp and lyre, praise him with tambourine and dancing, praise him with the strings and flute, praise him with the clash of cymbals, praise him with resounding cymbals' (Ps. 150:3–5). Here are strings, brass, woodwind and percussion. Instruments that play one note at a time, those that can harmonise several notes at once, and those that provide the rhythmic underlay. The sound must have been rich and rewarding to any lover of music.

We should also note the connection between tambourines and dancing. A similar link is made in another psalm: 'Let them praise his name with dancing and make music to him with tambourine and harp' (Ps. 149:3). This combination suggests that, in the great processions and within a worship service at the temple, some were appointed as dancers and accompanied their own movements by using tambourines. In the early days of Israel, all the women were sometimes called upon to dance: 'Then Miriam the prophetess, Aaron's sister, took a tambourine in her hand, and all the women followed her, with tambourines and dancing' (Exod. 15:20).

An individual Jew would sometimes use dance spontaneously in worship, notably David (2 Sam. 6:16). Jeremiah cited dance as one of the expressions of thankfulness and joy that would flow when God moved in saving power on the face of the earth: 'I will build you up again and you will be rebuilt, O Virgin Israel. Again you will take up your tambourines and go out to dance with the joyful' (Jer. 31:4). And, 'Then maidens will dance and be glad, young men and old as well. I will turn their mourning into gladness; I will give them comfort and joy instead of sorrow' (Jer 31:13). While dance is usually associated with women, it was clearly not seen as an exclusively female preserve. The Jews gave free and full expression, therefore, not only to the written arts of prose and poetry, but also to the performing arts of drama, music and dance.

The fine arts were also held in high esteem in ancient Israel. Bezalel son of Uri was chosen by God and filled with the Spirit in order to receive inspiration for his 'skill, ability and knowledge in all kinds of crafts – to make artistic designs for work in gold, silver and bronze, to cut and set stones, to work in wood, and to engage in all kinds of craftsmanship' (Exod. 31:2–5). The Old Testament therefore affirms that a person can receive a divine calling to work as an artist and that their artistry can be enhanced as they seek the inspiration of the Holy Spirit. In Moses' time, the ark of the covenant and the tent of meeting were not simply utilitarian. God gave skill to the craftsmen to create beautiful and ornate designs. In addition to the tent and altars, specialists were needed to create a pure gold lamp stand, the woven priestly garments of Aaron and his sons, and the precise blends of anointing oil and fragrant incense (Exod. 31:6–11). The worship of God was enhanced by beautiful sights, sounds and smells.

Solomon took Moses' willing encouragement of the arts to new heights when he built the first temple in Jerusalem. The dimensions of the temple are carefully recorded in the Old Testament, affirming the importance of the precise artistry of architecture. The stone-work was all finely dressed. The wood was the finest cedar, pine and olive. The metalwork was mainly bronze and gold. The artist in bronze was Hiram from Tyre, a non-Jew whose skill was re-nowned. His decorative work included human artefacts (chariot wheels, wreaths and interlocking chains); plant life (lilies, pome-granates and palm trees); and creatures, both natural and super-natural (lions, bulls and cherubim). The gold-work was lavish. Many artefacts were either made of gold or overlaid with gold, including an altar, a table, ten lamp stands, lamps and tongs, dishes, wick trimmers, sprinkling bowls, and golden sockets for the most prestigious temple doors (1 Kings 6–7). Perhaps the greatest surprise faced with such lavish artistry is that it only took seven years for the temple to be built.

Solomon had no time for bare walls and a roughly made, utili-tarian building. His temple could be summed up in the phrase: 'Nothing but the best.' In a primitive society, where living standards for most people could only have been very basic, to enter the temple would mean feasting your eyes upon a wonder of the ancient world. At considerable expense, Solomon used the finest artists and natural resources of the Middle East to construct a temple that gave dramatic visual expression to the magnificence of the living God. He was, therefore, not only the scientist king of ancient Israel, but a great promoter and patron of the arts. This great tradition of affirming the arts is seen in the history of Europe, where Christians have often been great artists and supporters of the arts.

We should not leave ancient Israel's support for the arts without mentioning three minor expressions of artistry: incense-making, cooking and gardening. Moses was given a specific recipe for the incense to be used in the Tent of Meeting, comprising equal amounts of gum resin, onycha, galbanum and pure frankincense.

The work was to be done by a skilled perfumer, and this particular recipe had to be kept exclusively for use in worship (Exod. 30:34–7). This affirms the place of the senses in worship – good smells to savour alongside good craftsmanship to see, and good words to sing. It also expresses appreciation for the craft of the perfumer and indicates that the use of incense was also a pleasurable part of domestic life, where a wide range of recipes were evidently enjoyed.

Related to the skills of the perfumer are those of the kitchen. The Jews understood worship in a very broad sense: not only did worship include sacrifices and fasts, it was also appropriate from time to time to feast in God's presence. Preparing and enjoying food were capable of being seen as spiritual activities, rather than being simply bodily distractions from our religious tasks. As to gardening, this was Adam's first job. Isaiah later used the picture of Israel as God's vineyard, which had failed to produce good fruit despite the gardener's best efforts (Isa. 5:1–7). And Jesus compared his followers with branches of a vine which his heavenly father would tend like a gardener (John 15). In short, not only does the Old Testament affirm a splendidly exuberant use of the major arts in the great public buildings of Israel, we can also discover affirmations of the domestic pleasures to be found in many different kinds of human artistry, including perfumery, cooking and gardening.

Until recently in Britain, perhaps the least appreciated art of all was storytelling. When I was at school, the study of English language included opportunities for creative writing, but at sixteen all such opportunities came to an end. The implication was clear: if you wanted to pursue something as unimportant as storytelling, you'd best do it in your own time instead of chasing girls and going to parties. Some chance!

Christians naturally admire Jesus as the greatest theologian of the New Testament, even amazing the temple experts when he was still a teenager. He is also the New Testament's greatest artist, the poet-preacher who captivated his audience with his unforgettable stories. Jesus' parables make great use of humour, including caricature and come-uppance for the mean-minded and vengeful. He uses the 'law of three', a traditional device of folk tales across the world, to lead his audience towards an expected climax to his story. He draws upon the everyday experience of peasants in Galilee –

losing coins, finding sheep, family arguments, owing money, sowing seed – which he must have observed carefully in order to be able to bring it to life so readily in his parables. He uses his imagination to convey eternal truth in stories that capture the imagination. The good news of the gospel takes earthy, everyday form in the parables of Jesus.

Sadly, many Christians have supposed that all truth is abstract. They would have preferred Jesus to write a systematic theology, a comprehensive account of Christian beliefs, rather than tell stories. As a result, many churches never encounter narrative preaching. And when we tackle Jesus' parables we quickly deconstruct them, stripping them of their imaginative force in order to identify 'what they are really about' as a series of abstract propositions. The gifts of the imagination and storytelling, enthusiastically affirmed in the ministry of Jesus, need urgently to be recovered among those who call themselves Jesus' disciples.

Turning back to Genesis 1, as well as establishing a theological framework for the doctrine of creation, we can also see this chapter as a highly wrought and imaginative hymn of creation. No word is out of place. The sense of rhythm and development is sustained with great eloquence. Genesis 1 celebrates the creativity of God in the shaping of the cosmos, and also his appreciation of artistry, when his pleasure in his creative work is repeatedly declared. To be made in the image of the Creator God means that we can understand our own creativity as a reflection of the divine creativity. We can share with God our pleasure in artistry, both our own and others'. Art needs no justification: it is a glorious gift of the Creator to those made in the divine image. Expressing our creativity is a way of glorifying God.

Art and discipleship

The history of art in Europe has been profoundly enriched for 2,000 years by Christians. Inevitably, not all Christian art is good art. Some of it has been very poor indeed, and some Christians have developed anti-art prejudices. But the Bible gives an unambiguous affirmation to creativity, however great or small our talents.

As we learn to release our artistry and our appreciation of art, we are giving fuller expression to the image of God. Christians therefore need to encourage artists of all kinds. We also need to affirm that you don't have to produce safe, conformist, middle-of-the-road, conventional art in order to be a faithful disciple. (Some Christian artists need protecting from over-zealous Christian philistines, who are robustly intolerant of anything that fails to conform to their own pedestrian tastes!) There is a cutting edge to God's creativity. There is a startling originality to some of the prophets' poems that made them deeply unpopular and easily misunderstood, just as the stark, even bleak, perspective of the book of Ecclesiastes is great poetry – but difficult to take for those who want their religion blithely optimistic, always effervescent and sunny side up. We can indeed, as T. S. Eliot once observed, only cope with very limited exposure to the harsher truths of human existence. We need Christians empowered in artistic expression of all kinds and at all levels, from high brow to mass market.

New technology opens up unprecedented opportunities for interaction between art and faith. Video projectors mean that we can incorporate into our services anything from an Old Master painting to video clips and PowerPoint presentations. Digital technology is constantly creating new opportunities for musical expression. Our buildings need to be properly wired for digital sound and multi-media. Many Christians are also quietly involved in painting or sculpture, poetry or prose, photography or flower arranging, playing an instrument or song-writing, cooking or gardening. As these talents are released to the full, our life experience and worship can be greatly enhanced. What a tragedy that many church buildings only become arts centres after they have been made redundant! If we took more seriously the discipleship of our creativity, our buildings could become inspirational centres of artistic expression, wonderfully attractive both to believers and non-believers.

If you have no time for anything creative, maybe you should pause a while to get back in touch with this aspect of what it means to be fully human. Finding an outlet for our own creativity and appreciating the creativity of others are both enormously beneficial if we are to explore the fullness of what it means to be made in the image of a Creator God. Becoming a disciple of Jesus Christ draws us into the redemptive relationship where God's image can begin to be restored in our lives. And that work of restoration will surely include discovering ways for our creativity to be rekindled by the incomparable creativity of God.

Chapter 6

Broken Image

THE FIRST TIME we were buying a house we could immediately see its full potential. Then we received the surveyor's report. I know that surveyors have to cover themselves against a client finding something wrong that they failed to report, but 'overkill' was obviously not in this surveyor's vocabulary. Nothing escaped his eye, from a slipped slate to woodworm, from a dodgy damp-proof course to a broken sash cord. By the time we had read to the page where the report drew our attention to a chipped tile in a fireplace surround that we had already destined for the scrapheap, it was hard to tell whether we felt more disillusioned with the house or with the surveying profession.

We have been exploring the incredibly rich and exciting implications of Genesis 1–2. The enormous variety of human potential finds its origins in the Creator – our spirituality and appreciation of the natural world, our capacity to find pleasure in work and rest, our ability to fall in love and sustain relationships, our scientific exploration and the gift of reason, our artistic expression and the gift of intuition. The psalmists expressed well the sheer wonder of human existence. One psalm declares that men and women are 'fearfully and wonderfully made' (Ps. 139:14). Another concludes that human beings are crowned with 'glory and honour' and made only a little lower than the angels (Ps. 8:5). Men and women are celebrated as God's masterpiece and the crown of creation.

Human potential deserves to be celebrated. When we recognise all that we have become and all that we could yet be, we are appreciating not only our own abilities but also God's handiwork. The Creator knew what he was doing and fashioned us to be a species capable of the most remarkable artistic, scientific and technological triumphs. That's why there is a long tradition of Christian humanism which celebrates the marvels of human accomplishment and potential. Those who believe in the Creator can afford to be generous in their appreciation of the ascent of man.

And yet, according to Genesis 3, this is only half the story. Made in the image of God, we now live out the consequences of the Fall. Our very existence is a blessing from God, and yet we also live under the curse of our own selfishness. Like an antique mirror that has cracked, we see the craftsmanship, but must live with a fatal flaw. The crown of creation has become the curse of creation. Made a little lower than the angels, we demean ourselves with selfish and destructive behaviour towards one another, whether in racial hatred, international wars, sporting rivalry or marital breakdown. If we are to grasp the full implications of our whole-life discipleship, we not only need to rediscover our potential in God's image, we must also face the much less optimistic realities of human sin and divine judgement. Genesis 3 traces five stages of human decline: the allure of temptation; giving in to sin; blaming one another; divine judgement; and exclusion from Eden. It is to this shadow side of human existence that we must now turn.

The tricks of temptation

The story of the Fall provides a profound insight and explanation of the innate contradictions of human existence. We find within ourselves an idealism that impels us towards self-improvement and a better society. And yet we cannot avoid the counter-influence of an instinctive selfishness that tends towards the failure of individuals to live up to their own ideals and the decline of society rather than the unhindered advance of civilisation. In millennium celebrations we are becoming familiar with these two faces of the human condition. On the one hand, our technology is advancing at an unprecedented rate so that we can now accomplish global communication and medical interventions that were inconceivable a hundred years ago, even to science fiction writers. At the same time, marriage survival is at an all time low, our sense of community is breaking down, and increasing fears are being expressed that many of today's children have little sense of right and wrong, no respect for any kind of authority, and little reason to expect to find any kind of love that lasts. At one and the same time, we are rising to new heights and falling apart at the seams.

Genesis traces this profound contradiction at the heart of human existence to our inability to say no when faced with temptation. Oscar Wilde once observed that he could resist everything except temptation. Mark Twain captured the perversity of the human heart by wryly suggesting that God should have allowed Adam and Eve to eat everything except the serpent, because then the tempter's eradication would have been almost immediate. With typical irony, Twain summed up the inner perversity that makes us feel that the only fruit really worth eating is one that has been forbidden.

When Genesis presents Adam and Eve's temptation and fall it provides a twofold analysis: first, how the inner contradiction of the human race arose; second, how we continue to make choices that draw us away from God and deeper into selfish and sinful living. According to Genesis, the essence of sin is disobedience to God, setting ourselves up as self-appointed gods in his place. Since some make such a strong connection between sin and sex we should also emphasise that there is no sexual aspect to the first temptation. To be sure, the impact of the Fall brings distortions to our sexual appetites, but this is equally true of sin's impact upon our every capacity and potential for good.

The series of observations made by the serpent to Eve provides a brilliant insight into the seductive power of temptation, both psychological and theological (Gen. 3:1–5). First, God is misrepresented. Permission had been granted for Adam and Eve to eat from every tree except one. But Satan recasts this restriction as a blanket statement of prohibition: 'You must not eat from any tree.' This is a common ploy in our society faced with any restriction on personal choices. The government-sponsored campaigns against AIDs in the West concentrated on 'safe sex'; that is, protected sex with as many partners as you want. A much healthier approach is found in the Bible: one partner, within marriage, for life. In the United States, there has been a widespread campaign among Christians to encourage young people to take a vow of celibacy until they are married. This is to be greatly applauded, since these youngsters are protecting themselves from physical disease and the potential emotional and psychological damage arising from casual sex. But some secular commentators immediately want to represent Christians as anti-sex. A sensible restriction that promotes healthy living is twisted into the appearance of total negativity.

This negative spin is designed to have two impacts. First, we are tempted to resent God, or those standing up for biblical morality, feeling that they are somehow robbing us of the freedom to indulge our natural appetites without restriction. We feel hard done by, as if God's requirements are unfair. Second, we are tempted to stand up for our rights, turning sinful indulgence into a crusading cause. Thus, for example, some of the champions of the decriminalisation of drugs and pornography speak as if all moral right were on their side, and that any kind of restriction on the sale and use of such things is by definition wrong.

Alongside the snide misrepresentation that seeks to portray God not as the generous Provider but rather as wilfully negative in his restriction of human freedom, Satan strikes another note in the phrase, 'Did God really say . . . ?' This is designed to introduce a note of uncertainty. An invitation is surreptitiously made to relativise God's command. Perhaps God didn't really mean it. Or perhaps we can interpret it differently. We have become sadly familiar in recent years with the sight of leading bishops appearing in the media to explain away biblical morality, preferring to take a stand for the immorality of today rather than the unchanging ethic of the Ten Commandments. Our society loves to relativise any claim to certainty and truth. The standard practice of television is to set two pundits against one another, whether two politicians, two scientists or a commercial representative and an eco-warrior. We are entertained by the sight and sound of combat by sound-bite. But the underlying impression is often that convictions are a matter of personal opinion and very little can ever be certain any more.

Eve's first response is fairly resilient. Perhaps it would have been better not to engage in this conversation at all. It is certainly the case today, with all manner of temptations, that the best thing is to close a conversation and walk away quickly from the snare. The longer you talk, the greater the risk that the trap will be sprung. Eve reasserts a positive view of God's law – they can eat of all the trees except one, and that tree must not be touched on pain of death.

Unfortunately, even as Eve resists temptation, she begins to make allowances for the tempter's perspective. God had emphasised the positive more strongly than Eve – 'You are free to eat from any tree' compared with 'We may eat fruit from the trees'. Eve describes God not as 'the Lord God', which is the standard way of referring to God in this narrative, but simply as 'God', which is the same name used by the tempter. What's more, Eve embellished God's warning that eating of the forbidden fruit would lead to death: in her account, just to touch it would prove fatal. Here is a telling dynamic of temptation. The more weak willed and compliant we are, the more inclined we will be to make allowances for our tempter's perspective, watering down our own convictions or having our values unconsciously infiltrated by the language and emphases we are trying to resist.

The serpent quickly develops his attack. First he dismisses the threat of death – 'You will surely not die.' There clearly have been times when well-intentioned people have greatly exaggerated the dire consequences of breaking their moral code. Financial ruin, family breakdown, blindness and deafness have all been held out as the dread and direct consequence of indulging the forbidden actions. When the boundaries are tested and the threatened consequences do not immediately follow, the entire moral framework is discredited and is at risk of being dismissed out of hand.

While moral prudes invent mythical dangers, those with an immorality to market will dismiss risks that are real. 'No harm can come of it' is the cry, of the pimp coaxing a girl into a new line of work, of the drug pusher offering tablets at a rave, of the business-man pressing a colleague into a shady deal, of the impatient man pressing unprotected sex on his inexperienced girlfriend, and of the housebreaker who explains to himself that his victims won't really suffer because they can claim everything back on insurance.

The serpent follows up immediately on the insinuation that the dangers of immorality have been greatly exaggerated. He brings his arguments to a climax with a double assault. He appeals to human ambition, with the promise that the fruit will make them like gods. And he implies that the real reason for the restriction is not to protect men and women, but rather for God to preserve his own exclusive rights to divinity. The subtlety of temptation must be heeded. Satan nowhere attempts a direct instruction or appeal to eat the forbidden fruit. His task is to ensnare, his methods are indirect, as he seeks to construct a context in which it feels as if the natural next step is to embrace immorality. All too often, where a direct assault would fail, an indirect approach sneaks behind our defences before we even realise the moral danger.

The power of temptation is beguiling. However, Adam and Eve have not yet sinned. And the tempter cannot make them sin. He can make disobedience seem trivial – 'It really won't matter at all.' Or he can make it sound a once-in-a-lifetime opportunity – 'Let the end justify the means. Reach for the stars and become all that you can be.' He can encircle them with arguments and promises. But the choice is still theirs. And the same, of course, is true for each one of us when we face our daily dose of temptations.

The serpent's arguments remain alluring and in frequent use today. Biblical morality is misrepresented as narrow, negative and life-denying. Relativism rejects the idea of moral absolutes and tries to explain away any restrictions we don't like. It is claimed that immorality is no more than harmless fun, and illegality need cause no alarm because the chances of getting caught are slender. The appeal to ambition promises that we will be more fulfilled, more successful or more powerful if we compromise our moral convictions. Sin, it is promised, will actually do us good. And the serpent's slur against God usually becomes an attack on religious leaders, politicians or judges, who are dismissed as hypocrites, imposing rules on others that they flagrantly breach themselves.

There is no immunity from temptation. After all, Jesus himself was tempted, yet remained pure. When we do give in to selfish instincts, forgiveness in Christ is freely available whenever we repent. But the quickest and most fulfilling way to deal with temptation is much more direct and always the same, whatever kind of temptation we happen to be facing. Just say no.

The dynamics of sin

Just as we can trace several facets of temptation in Genesis 3 that are familiar from today's world and our individual life experiences, this chapter continues its remarkable and profound insights into the human condition by analysing the dynamics of giving in to temptation. When the serpent finished speaking, the active choices of disobedience were yet to be made by Adam and Eve. The tempter's arguments were designed to nullify God's law. And then the tempted duo began to discover a deepening allure in the forbidden fruit. Even so, whenever we follow the path they took, we will find ourselves ever more likely to make harmful moral choices, sliding into disobedience and selfishness.

Before we explore this dynamic, we should clear up a couple of misconceptions. The first is the assumption that the fruit was an apple – the precise species of fruit that was forbidden is not actually specified. The whole point of the prohibition seems to have been to provide an opportunity for moral freedom and genuine obedience. Without the capacity to make genuine moral choices, life may have been easier, but we would not be truly free or fully human.

The second misconception is that Adam was elsewhere at the time of the temptation. Some chauvinists have tried to suggest that Eve should have been preparing a meal at home rather than wandering around the garden. Others have attempted to lay most or all of the blame on Eve, as if the Fall was all her fault and Adam merely joined in later. But the text is quite explicit: at the time of the temptation, Adam and Eve were together (Gen. 3:6). Adam made no attempt to intervene in the confrontation with the serpent, nor did he try to prevent Eve from harvesting the forbidden fruit. She took the fruit from the tree and Adam took it from her. Just as they were partners in tending the garden, they were partners in sin. Neither was an innocent party or a junior accomplice: both made moral choices and both were equally at fault.

First, Eve decides that the fruit is 'good for food'. Her first attraction is impulsive and physical. Perhaps her mouth may have begun to water at the prospect of savouring such delicious flesh.

Second, Eve finds it 'pleasing to the eye'. The longer Eve's gaze lingers on the fruit, the less likely she is to resist temptation. Since every other kind of fruit was freely available, there was plenty else upon which to feast her eyes. But she quickly comes to the point where she only has eyes for one fruit. Here we can detect a shift from a moment of physical attraction to a deeper sense of craving as she continues to dwell on the incomparable attractiveness of this particular kind of fruit.

Third, Eve finds it 'desirable for gaining wisdom'. She moves beyond the prospect of enjoying the fruit in itself to the hope of benefiting from its consumption in some deeper way. She is now drawing the conclusion that the act of disobedience will somehow make her a better person. We can trace this motivation in many experiences. Some 'just want to know what it would be like', while others feel they have something to prove. For example, the peer pressures on teenagers to lose their virginity, try illegal drugs, take up smoking, drink under age and swear like a trooper can all carry overtones not only of being in the in-crowd, but of somehow qualifying, winning our spurs, as a fully fledged young adult. Not that temptations cease at eighteen or twenty-one. Throughout life we continue to face temptation. And the same spiral of attraction continues: an initial moment of attraction, a lingering gaze, and then a growing conviction that somehow we will become a better or more fulfilled person if only we give in to temptation.

Once the dynamic of giving in to temptation is complete, actions are swift. In an instant, Eve takes the fruit and eats it, then promptly gives some to Adam who eats without delay. It's much safer and easier to say no as early as possible during the process of temptation. By the time the forbidden fruit is within our grasp, it's so much harder to walk away.

Genesis gives us an insight into Eve's interior life, but not Adam's. Maybe he had none, and was a much less complex, more immediate kind of person. With little reflection or awareness of the dynamics of temptation he was faced with an opportunity to sin and he just took it. Act on impulse and face up to the consequences later. On the other hand, maybe Adam faced an equivalent struggling with sin, but the writer of Genesis 3 wanted to avoid repetition. Either way, Adam is without excuse. If he struggled within, he failed. If he acted on impulse, his behaviour was just as wrong. Whatever the circumstances that lead up to our disobedience, when we cross the boundary of God's law we are in the wrong and will inevitably have to answer for our offence.

Living under judgement

Just as Genesis 3 provides us with penetrating and practical insights into the dynamics of temptation, it also explores the destructive consequences of sin. The immediate impact is that both Adam's and Eve's eyes are opened to their own nakedness and they make some primitive clothing. Previously they had enjoyed the innocent liberty of being naked and unashamed. Now they are no longer comfortable with the sight of their own bodies. Uncomfortable with themselves and one another, they then make feeble attempts to hide from God. Like shamefaced children who behave awkwardly when they have been caught red-handed, Adam and Eve reluctantly own up to their disobedience.

As God questions the foolish couple, they make feeble efforts to pass off the blame (Gen. 3:12–13). Adam speaks first and tries to pin the blame on Eve and God. On Eve, because he emphasises that it was she who took the fruit and gave it to him to eat. And on God, because he was the One who had given Eve to Adam in the first place. In her turn, Eve tries to pass the buck to Satan. These defences have been heard on countless lips, both children and adults – 'She did it first!' and 'You should never have put me in such a risky situation!' and 'I had no choice, the pressures were so great that I just had to give in!' Adam and Eve have yet to come to terms with an inescapable reality: before the judgement seat of God, the buck always stops with the guilty party.

In these immediate responses we see a new factor in human existence: alienation. Adam and Eve are alienated from their own bodily existence, and so they hide themselves self-consciously. As they try to avoid the consequences of their disobedience, their attempts at self-justification collide with God's gifts of freedom and responsibility. And as Adam pins the blame on Eve and even on God, we see that selfish actions lead to hostility and accusation, dividing us from one another and from the Creator. Before the Fall, God's creation was characterised by harmony and wholeness. As a result of disobedience, we are faced with discord, the breakdown of relationships, and isolation.

God's spoken judgements reinforce this new experience of alienation (Gen. 3:14–19). The joy of having children will be tempered by increased pain in childbirth. The joy of the marriage relationship will be tarnished by destructive tendencies. The woman's 'desire' will be for her husband. That could mean that her sexual appetite will be difficult to control or satisfy. It could mean that she will long for mastery over her husband, for they will now function more as rivals than partners. Or it could mean that she will want to be with him come what may, which certainly seems to be the fate of some battered women, who seem unable to escape from a destructive relationship. It may well be that all of these implications are encompassed in these words of divine judgement.

At the same time, the man will now 'rule over the woman'. To love and to cherish becomes to dominate and to crave. The tyranny of male domination in all its forms is not a gift of creation, but a symptom of the Fall: murder and rape, wife battering and child abuse, using prostitutes, treating women as sex objects, patronising women as sub-standard beings with the implication that they are incapable of intelligent thought or sporting prowess, or leadership in politics and business. In these and so many other ways men have an innate tendency to demean women, and in so doing we also demean ourselves.

God's judgement on Adam and Eve finds continued expression today in many experiences of mutual misunderstanding, rivalry and enmity. Genesis describes the paradoxes of love that have been the subject ever since of plays and poems, novels and films. The creative and life-enhancing experiences of human love can be contaminated and even undermined by selfish instincts and mutually destructive appetites. The optimism and hope of the marriage day all too often wither and fade with the passing of years as selfishness and rejection accumulate and young love becomes a distant memory. The sex wars that are fought today in the acrimony of the divorce courts, in jokes that make a mockery of the opposite sex, and in sex discrimination cases, found their origin in the fall of the human race.

Three further judgements are also imposed upon the human race. First, the ground is cursed, so that work is now degraded into 'painful toil' requiring much hard labour, and thorns and thistles will proliferate as a sign of divine displeasure. In our weariness at the end of a busy week, work can easily seem somehow less than we feel it could be, even in the most fulfilling of careers.

Second, we live with the inevitability of our own mortality. Created as composite beings, material and yet spiritual, from earthly dust and divine breath, we will live with the unpalatable knowledge that our body is destined to return to the dust. Not until Jesus' resurrection from the dead could there be any confidence in the prospect of life beyond the grave. Death has become the 'last obscenity' in the United Kingdom today, the one topic that no one will raise in polite company. It's usually left to great artists in their more morose moments to explore for us the dread prospect of our own demise.

Third, Adam and Eve are expelled from the garden, to which they can find no return. This sense of being not quite at home in our present existence often finds expression today – 'There must be more to life than this!' We carry with us an intuitive sense of a greater, more beautiful and harmonious existence, where wholeness has not been usurped by fragmentation, and where we could experience oneness rather than division in relating to one another and to ourselves, to God, and to the glories of creation. We have become refugees in search of home. The new Eden will be found in heaven itself, where there will be no more divisions and enmity, no more toil or mortality, because neither sin nor its destructive consequences will be allowed entry.

Human existence, according to Genesis 1–3, cannot be understood adequately until we grasp that we have become an amalgam of creative potential and destructive selfishness. Men and women are at one and the same time the crown of creation and its curse. In the nobility of the divine image we can enhance the glory of creation, and in our fallenness we bring to the song of creation a terrible discord. Those who celebrate the image without facing up to the sinfulness become naively optimistic and utopian. Those who spell out the ugly consequences of our innate sinfulness without celebrating the gift of the divine image become broodingly apocalyptic and can see no good in human beings at all. To understand our potential and our failings, we must grasp hold of the truth that we have been made in the image of God and yet take account of the instinctive sinfulness of the human heart. The divine image is neither annulled nor unsullied. The image is present in every human being, but broken in all.

Only in Christ can we see the undisfigured image of God, without any tarnish of sin. As disciples of Christ we seek the gradual restoration of the divine image in our lives. To become more like Christ is to begin to fulfil our original potential. Whole-life discipleship holds out the promise of a life that can become very good indeed.

Part Two
Restoring the Image

Chapter 7

Springboard of Hope

THE FIRST TIME you use a gymnastics springboard it can be a strange experience. It somehow doesn't seem right to jump down in order to leap up. The New Testament often speaks about faith, hope and love. These are three pivotal Christian qualities that we all need to develop. At the beginning of his letter to the Colossians Paul explains that faith and love can be uplifted by the springboard of hope. The more we are grounded in authentic biblical hope, the higher we can leap into faith and love.

The Church has not always kept to the biblical springboard. Sometimes it has looked as if denominational authorities have wanted to take away the springboard altogether, producing annual reports that are full of nothing but defeatism and decline. Enthusiastic Christians are more likely to be tempted to replace the biblical springboard with something that looks more exciting and up to date, but this can lead to our building upon expectations that are only loosely connected with the teaching of the New Testament. Leaders and speakers can be over-promoted, indulging a cult of personality. We can oversell a denomination, new or old, as if our grouping had all the right answers, a monopoly of biblical structures and insights, and our glorious triumph was assured. We can oversell particular gifts and styles of worship, turning a particular spiritual gift or way of praying into a cure-all, or making our preferred style of worship a narrow and compulsory bill of fare for every believer. We can overstate the growth of the Church in the West, creating a 'just around the next corner' mind-set. This can be very exciting in the short term, but eventually the credibility of any exaggerated claim is sure to wear thin. The heralds of false dawns must not be surprised if eventually people stop listening to them. Enthusiastic hype is a poor substitute for genuine, biblical hope.

False hope makes the heart sick. A cynic is often a disappointed idealist. When fanciful and unrealistic dreams are dashed, we can lurch to the opposite extreme and find it difficult to keep hold of any kind of optimism or expectancy. Once we have believed too much, the swing of the pendulum can leave us finding it easier to believe and hope for almost nothing any more. The secure foundation for effective discipleship is certainly not defeatism, but nor is it found in extravagant hype, intoxicating for a season but ultimately disappointing. What then is the authentic springboard of biblical hope? Paul identifies five factors. We can picture them as five springs which together comprise the strong and reliable springboard of the biblical hope that will never fail and can always bring us fresh inspiration.

Dead-end discipleship

Before we explore these five factors, we will first identify the Colossian hang-ups that were holding them back from Christian maturity and effective discipleship. When I was a child, we had a family saying that if my father attempted to find a short cut, we were sure to end up in a dead end. Even so, throughout the history of the Church, Christians have attempted to find short cuts in discipleship which can seem attractive at first but end up going nowhere. The dead ends the Colossians were facing have often ensnared Christians ever since. Someone once said that those who refuse to learn from the past are condemned to repeat its mistakes. The Colossians can help us to avoid the dead ends of false spirituality and failed discipleship, if only we are willing to learn from their confusion.

In order to identify the Colossian hang-ups we have to do some detective work, since we don't have a straightforward listing of the teaching that was bogging them down. Their problems become apparent through the things to which Paul gives special emphasis. We can readily trace four strands: 1 super-spirituality; 2 religious regulations; 3 food and drink rules; 4 muddle-headed doctrines.

1 Super-spirituality

This has always been a problem for Christians. Since we believe in a supernatural God, we cannot exclude unusual supernatural experiences. Paul himself was converted through an astonishing encounter with the risen Christ, which caused him to fall to the ground and left him temporarily blind (Acts 9). Later, he described an occasion in the temple precincts when he fell into a trance and was warned to leave Jerusalem quickly (Acts 22:17–18). He also reported, though rather reluctantly and obliquely, a remarkable vision of what he called the 'third heaven' (2 Cor. 12:1–5). Because we want to be open to spiritual realities, there is always a risk of gullibility, with keen Christians being taken for a ride by someone whose claimed experiences become ever more exotic and elaborate. For the Colossians, this common problem took the form of visions of angels. The Colossians took the reality of these spiritual beings so seriously that they began to divert some of their worship from God. The keenest exponents of this self-styled 'higher spirituality' went into elaborate detail about their visions. As a result, the Colossians were in awe of the visionaries and started to chase after angelic visions for themselves.

Paul and his fellow apostles were not against angels. How could they be when an angel had announced the birth of Christ (Luke 1:26) and prepared the way for mission to the Gentiles (Acts 10:3). But Paul makes a clear distinction between authentic angels and people who talk about angels a great deal to elevate their own spiritual status. His own reticence about describing his spiritual experiences was because he wanted no one to think more highly of him than his words and talk deserved (2 Cor. 12:6). This is a refreshing contrast to some high-profile international ministries today that are forever elaborating their own latest revelatory encounters with the risen Christ.

So far as Paul was concerned, despite their claims to great humility, those who never stopped talking about angels were full of idle notions that puffed them up with conceit (Col. 2:18). Far from being taken in by their claims to a higher spirituality, Paul dismissed them as having minds that were 'unspiritual'. Super-spirituality can take many forms, and will often seem very impressive at face value. But we should not be taken in. Far from being a higher spirituality as it claims, the truth about super-spirituality is that it's a lot less spiritual than real Christian discipleship.

2 Religious regulations

These were well-loved by the Pharisees. Faced with Jesus healing on a Saturday, they were more concerned about a breach of the Sabbath law than the benefits for the person who had just received a miracle. The human spirit seems instinctively more comfortable with patterns of religion that weave a web of strict regulations rather than staying with the true Christian freedom of unadorned faith. Legalism has been able to infect almost every expression of Christianity over the centuries. Today's informal customs become tomorrow's legalistic obligations. All too easily we become obsessed with outward things and quickly learn to disapprove of any Christians who fail to fall into line with our religious code of conduct. In previous generations, well-intentioned Christians have completely 'lost the plot' of New Testament discipleship by banning toys or television on Sundays or making formal clothes compulsory at worship services, as if the risen Christ would not respond to a woman dressed in jeans or a man not wearing a tie.

The Colossians were getting sucked into a strange hotch-potch of Jewish and Gentile religious observances, setting aside all manner of religious festivals, Sabbath days and new moon celebrations (Col. 2:16). Paul's repudiation of such observances certainly does not mean that dedicated disciples should staunchly refuse to celebrate Christmas or birthdays, or any festivals of spring, summer and autumn. Paul is not promoting a negative attitude to life, he is trying to release the Colossians from all such distortions of true discipleship. Freedom and joy in the grace of Christ had been usurped by an endless routine of religious obligations. Living as disciples had been distorted by a treadmill of regulations designed to win and retain God's favour. Paul sets up a stark contrast: such things are a mere foreshadowing of the gift of salvation that has now been made available in Christ (Col. 2:17). In the same way that many of us will have bought an upgrade of computer software from an earlier version to which we will never have a reason to return, when we come to faith in

Christ we have discovered the ultimate spiritual reality, and thus there's no reason to go back to the old ways. To downgrade to the religious practices of the Pharisees, in legalism and negativity, no matter how much such things are approved in some churches, is pointless and foolish according to the New Testament. Far from tying us in legalistic knots, whole-life discipleship is meant to bring us into an experience of liberation in the grace of Christ.

3 Food and drink rules

Just as the Pharisees loved religious days where duty came before love, they also developed elaborate food and drink rules. Jesus repudiated such an approach to holiness, explaining that what makes us unclean is not our food, which merely passes through us, but the selfish and destructive behaviour that issues from our inmost being. Paul had just as little time for food laws. The Colossians were clearly accustomed to a detailed set of dietary restrictions – 'Do not handle! Do not taste! Do not touch!' (Col. 2:21). Paul's response is to tell them that they should not let anyone judge them by what they ate or drank (Col. 2:16).

Paul acknowledged that the dedication of those who adhere to a strict regime of food and drink laws can seem impressive at first sight (Col. 2:23), but he dismissed food laws on two counts. First, such rules belong to this world, are based on human commands and teachings, and are destined to pass away (Col. 2:20–2). That is, they are expressions of human religion that have nothing to do with the Christian gospel and true discipleship. Second, this harsh treatment of the body is ultimately worthless (Col. 2:23). According to Paul, strict dietary rules never made any difference to human character and are powerless to restrain sensual indulgence. In other words, you can leave countless kinds of food and drink out of your diet and still be the same person. Character improvement requires inner spiritual renewal rather than a strictly controlled diet. For as long as the Colossians were food obsessed, their diet was centre stage and they were completely missing the point about the cross of Christ and the power of the Spirit to bring about genuine inner change.

4 Muddle-headed doctrines

Behind poor practice is usually poor doctrine. The Colossians seem to have succumbed to the standard Greek prejudice of their day that took for granted that spirit and matter were like oil and water: they simply could not mix. This conviction had three natural results. First, the body was seen as marginal to spirituality, something to be punished and disciplined and generally got out of the way of the human spirit. We see this reflected in the rules and regulations Paul seeks to lift off the backs of the Colossians.

Second, since God is the purest form of spirit, it was thought that he could not deal directly with the material world. The Greeks developed the notion of a kind of ladder of spiritual beings descending from God to the earth: the less spiritual the beings, the closer they could get to the material world. Once the Colossians took these spiritual beings seriously, they began to wonder whether they deserved worship in their own right. This is reflected in Paul's reference to angel worship. However, when Paul celebrates the creation of the cosmos, he emphatically declares that everything has been created by God, without any kind of reliance on lesser spiritual beings. He lists several kinds of spiritual forces that the Colossians were presumably taking very seriously – 'thrones or powers or rulers or authorities' (Col. 1:16) – and insists that they were all created by the pre-existent Christ and for his pleasure. (We'll come back to the cosmic Christ in Chapter 10.) God's work of creation is direct, and every created being is subordinate to Christ and cannot deserve the worship due only to God.

Paul once again emphasises the unique authority of Christ when he explains that all malevolent 'powers and authorities' were disarmed at the cross (Col. 2:15). Faced with Christians who were taking these intermediate spiritual beings too seriously, Paul is at pains to stress the total supremacy of Christ. Good spiritual beings don't need to be worshipped, for they are totally dependent upon God for their existence. The hostile ones don't need to be placated, for they have been totally subjugated by the cross of Christ.

Third, this Greek prejudice had great difficulty coping with the incarnation of Christ as the God-man, fully divine and yet fully human. The dualistic assumptions of Greek thought made two extreme theories attractive: either Christ was truly God and only took on the appearance of human form or Christ was truly human and was adopted by God as his son, because he had made such a good job of living a life of love. These two denials stayed attractive to those schooled in Greek thought for several hundred years and became known as docetism, which means Christ only seemed to be human, and adoptionism, which means Christ was no more than a good man. John's Gospel was written for people influenced by this Greek way of thinking, and the first chapter tackles these prejudices head on. First, John celebrates the Son of God as the Logos, a Greek term signifying God's wisdom, the mind which orders the cosmos. First-century Gentiles would have been reassured that John was a theologian talking their kind of language, but then he introduced a distinctive and radically new element of Christian conviction: 'The Word *became flesh* [my italics] and lived for a while among us. We have seen his glory . . .' (John 1:14).

According to conventional Greek thinking, this was an absurdity. But John is not developing a new philosophical theory, he is describing an event. For John, the only reasonable explanation of the most decisive moment in human history is that in Christ we see the human face of God. The spiritual and the material worlds have been yoked together in the miracle of the incarnation.

Paul takes up this same theme in his letter to the Colossians: 'For God was pleased to have all his fulness dwell in him' (Col. 1:19). And, 'For in Christ all the fulness of the Deity lives in bodily form' (Col. 2:9). The statements are emphatic, combining 'all' with 'fulness'. The repetition is insistent. Paul is evidently countering a hesitation among the Colossians. The incarnation is not partial, it is total. The revelation is not provisional, it is final. The integration of the divine and human is not illusory or fragmentary, it happened fully, freely and definitively. Paul is facing a group of believers who are wondering whether true discipleship requires Christ plus something else: angel worship, religious festivals, food and drink laws. His response is uncompromising: if they want to embrace true Christianity and commit themselves to effective discipleship, all they need is Jesus Christ.

This old Greek division between body and spirit has cast long shadows over the attitudes of the Western Church. We can still meet Christians who think that the material world is a distraction from being really spiritual and that our bodies just get in the way. On top of this ancient prejudice, more recent cultural convictions have brought their own distortions to the gospel. The enlightenment placed such an emphasis on rationality that some Christians have become instinctively suspicious of any experience of God or emotional dimension of living faith. Late twentieth-century existentialism has swung to the opposite extreme. Like characters in a *Star Wars* movie, some Christians behave as if it's best not to think at all and just use their instincts. At these equal and opposite extremes, Christians become dogmatically anti-intuitive or anti-intellectual. Both attitudes are rooted, however unconsciously, more in cultural prejudices than in the Scriptures.

Paul's account of dead-end discipleship is sure to come as a shock to some Christians. We may not have come across angel worship and theories about different levels of spiritual beings, but many of us will have come across super-spirituality of some kind and also legalistic attitudes, often reflected in a concern with special religious days or prohibitions on various kinds of food and drink. Enthusiastic young Christians are very likely to suppose that really committed disciples are very particular about their diet, pay careful attention to religious festivals, and have wonderful visionary experiences to recount at regular intervals. But Paul will have none of it. He insists that true discipleship will liberate us from the burdens of petty legalism and the flights of fancy of super-spirituality. Paul therefore called the Colossians to a fundamental choice that we must also face: the excesses of legalism and exotic visions, or the reality of spiritual maturity as a true disciple of Christ.

The five springs of hope

For a couple of years there has been a building site on the way to my sons' school. Only recently has it been possible for the untrained eye to see what kind of building they are constructing. In the long months of laying foundations, progress seemed painfully slow. Suddenly the construction is racing ahead and the date of opening is displayed outside. It's easy to forget the foundations now that they can no longer be seen, but they were absolutely essential for the success of the whole project. In a similar way, when Paul identifies five crucial elements of our hope in Christ, he is spelling out the totally dependable foundations upon which our discipleship can be built.

1 The power of the cross

Paul sums up the gospel as 'God's grace in all its truth' (Col. 1:6). He never tires of celebrating the centrality and saving power of the cross. God's great work of reconciliation is accomplished by 'making peace through his blood, shed on the cross' (Col. 1:20). We can come before the Father without blemish and free from accusation because of the death of Christ's physical body (Col. 1:22). The written code that was against us has been taken away, and is now nailed to the cross (Col. 2:14). The hostile spiritual powers and authorities have been defeated at the cross (Col. 2:15). We shall explore the impact of the cross more fully in Chapter 9, but for now we need to affirm its centrality to the gospel, and therefore in our worship and proclamation. The cross is the place where God's work of salvation is completed. The cross is the pivotal event of human history, the once-for-all moment of atonement. The fact of the cross and resurrection, written on the pages of human history, can give us confidence in every circumstance of life that the grace of God will prevail and saving love will triumph in the end.

2 The authority of the Word

Paul speaks of the word of truth, which is the gospel (Col. 1:5). The preached word of the first apostles declared the living Word of the Son of God. And their preached word became, in turn, the basis for the written Word of the Scriptures. God continues to speak to us, particularly through preaching and prophecy, but his definitive self-revelation is in the person of his Son, and his primary means of communication with us is through the Bible.

My life has been full of books. As a student of English and

related literature at university, I bought my own copies of many of the classics. As a publisher, I collected many more books. As a Christian minister, books continue to play a vital part in my profession. Many years ago we were moving house and members of our home group lent us a hand. One was a self-employed handyman who had probably not read many books since leaving school. He took me on one side to give me some fatherly advice. 'What I find,' he explained, 'is that it's generally best to throw away a book once you have finished reading it.' To us bookaholics, that is near blasphemy! As I write, there are bookshelves in my study, our lounge, dining room and garage. You will gather I am very fond of my books. None the less, I have never encountered any book like the Bible. It's not just bursting with insights into how to live well, it's a book with an extra dimension. The presence of God can be found in its pages. It has a unique authority and a unique capacity to get under people's skin with rebukes, encouragement, and life-enriching inspiration. Paul explained the supreme authority of the Bible: this is no mere compilation of human writings, in a unique way the holy Scriptures are God-breathed (2 Tim. 3:16).

3 The reality of personal conversion

Paul writes confidently that the gospel has been growing among the Colossians ever since the day they heard and understood God's grace (Col. 1:6). According to statistics, about one-third of professing Christians can put a definite date on their conversion: everything fell into place for them so clearly that they made a definite response of faith and were decisively born again. The other two-thirds experience a period of overlap, a time when they are making a journey towards personal faith, but are not yet sure whether they have really come through. For them, conversion is more of a process than a one-stop experience. This can be equally true for some with believing parents, who may grow into the faith from earliest childhood days, and also for some who discover Christianity for themselves later in life. For myself, I can look back to a time when I was definitely not a believer, and that time was followed by a period of uncertain transition for two or three years. By the end of that time I knew I had become a Christian, but I could not possibly pinpoint a single, decisive moment during that interim phase.

The important thing, according to the New Testament, is not that we can set a date on our conversion, but that we know we have been converted. The fact that we have been forgiven, justified, adopted, reconciled, and welcomed for all eternity into God's new family of love, establishes a crucial foundation for Christian hope that is secure. Otherwise we may find ourselves endlessly repeating prayers of commitment, just in case. If that's where you are right now, I urge you to speak with a mature Christian in your church. As you talk and pray together, you too can break through to a confident faith. I know because I have been there, and now I am confident that I have given my life to Jesus Christ and am secure in his love for all eternity.

4 The promise of heaven

We can look back in hope to the cross and our own conversion, and we can also look forward in expectancy. Paul speaks of hope 'stored up' in heaven (Col. 1:5). It's not that we can begin to store up our reward by living the right kind of life. Instead, God's eternal love is already held on deposit in our name. I frequently get letters from the *Reader's Digest* explaining how lucky I am to be one of the privileged few in south-west London to be entered for their latest prize draw. To emphasise that the prize is genuine, they invariably state that the money is already stored on deposit, just waiting for the draw to be made. There's no lucky draw for heaven. God's love is stored up not for one fortunate winner, but for everyone who puts their trust in Christ. If we worked our passage to heaven, our reward in heaven could only be determined at the end of our life. But this is a promise of grace: the lavish riches of God's grace in Christ are already stored up for every believer. The resurrection of Christ has demonstrated that death is not the end of life, but the beginning of the next phase. Once we have put our trust in Christ we can live in the light of our sure and certain hope. Whatever else may happen in life, ultimately we are heaven-bound and the best is yet to come.

5 The advance of the Church

Paul encourages the Colossians with the fact that the gospel is bearing fruit throughout the known world (Col. 1:6). Despite his own imprisonment, the mistaken emphases of the Colossian church, the continuing indifference and ignorance of most people in the city of Colosse and throughout the Empire, and the fact that the authorities were largely untouched and unimpressed by the first Christians, Paul is able to declare an enduring confidence in the gospel. The reason is simple. The gospel is nothing less than the power of God, and the God who raised Christ Jesus from the dead is perfectly capable not merely of protecting but also of advancing his Church across the world.

At the dawn of the twenty-first century, the worldwide Church is growing faster than ever in its history. The Church in Western Europe needs reminding of this world context as we work and pray to turn around a century of numerical decline. Tertullian, an apologist in the early Church, confidently repudiated the Roman Empire's attempts to exterminate Christianity, declaring that the blood of the martyrs is the seed of the Church. Beza, a Reformation leader, reminded the king of France that the Church was an anvil that had worn out many hands. G. K. Chesterton once observed that several times in its history the Church seemed to be going to the dogs, and every time it was the dog that died. The ruthless persecutions of the Soviet Union ended not with the extinction of Christianity, but the collapse of communism. There is divine and resurrection power in the gospel and the Church of Jesus Christ, which is demonstrated in the continuing advance of the worldwide Church. In the decadent and paganised West, this gives us great encouragement and inextinguishable hope as we work for the rebirth of the Church in the twenty-first century.

This fivefold foundation provides us with the springboard of hope – the power of the cross, the authority of the Word, the reality of our personal conversion, the promise of heaven, and the worldwide advance of the gospel. We are sustained in the present by the decisive events of the past and the certain promises of our future in Christ. This is enduring hope, sure and real, stable and lasting.

Inspired by this springboard of totally reliable hope, our spirits can be lifted as we seek to be faithful followers of Christ, eagerly pursuing the path of lifelong discipleship.

Chapter 8

Fulfil Your Potential

Colossians 1:9–12

I LOVE TO GO walking in the Lake District. There's something irresistibly glorious about that ancient and majestic landscape. And it's remarkably easy to get off the beaten track and enjoy time without a valley-loving tourist in sight. The guidebooks invariably provide a huge list of things you need to take with you for a safe day in the fells. A warm jumper and waterproofs, a map and a compass, a whistle and a first aid kit, a torch and a protective sheet in case you need to make an overnight shelter – the list goes on and one. But above all else, you need to take emergency supplies of Kendal mint cake. I love the stuff and live in the happy knowledge that my wife hates it, so I have to eat her portion just to be sure that we are both safe! In fact, I sometimes wonder whether the chief reason for going to the Lake District is so that we can have an excuse to enjoy plenty of bars of mint cake!

This exhaustive list of supplies is said to be necessary for a safe and rewarding day in the hills. Likewise, the New Testament reveals God's resources for effective discipleship. When Paul writes down his prayer for the Colossians he is providing more than a well-turned phrase. This letter found its way into the Scriptures because it has that something extra which is the inspiration of the Spirit. Paul's prayer is therefore timeless, as relevant to us as to the first-century Colossians. More than that, it is revelatory, making plain to us not only Paul's prayer for the Colossians but also the risen Christ's best purposes for his Church in every generation. What, then, are the resources that God wants to bestow upon his Church for effective discipleship?

A renewed mind

Paul prays that we will grow in the knowledge of God's will (Col. 1:9). A renewed mind is not merely speculative or theoretical. This knowledge will lead to practical obedience, and Paul explains that it comes about in two ways, through wisdom and understanding. Wisdom means insight; that is, learning how to make sense of life more deeply. We can sum up wisdom as learning to look at the world from God's perspective. I never cease to be amazed by encyclopedias on CD-ROM. An entire shelf of books can be compressed on to a single silver disk. And now a new generation of encyclopedias are being made available via the Internet. Information has never been so freely, widely and quickly available. It's a great privilege, unknown to previous generations. However, the one thing you cannot find in any kind of encyclopedia is wisdom. It comes about as a gift of God and by prayerful reflection on life in the light of our study of the Bible.

Understanding means being able to discern the next step to take, whether in our careers or at home. God wants to help us make good choices with the key decisions in our lives. Wisdom provides the overview. Understanding helps with the details. And both, according to Paul, are gifts of God as he works on the renewal of our minds.

Paul adds a crucial detail by describing this wisdom and understanding as 'spiritual'. That means the renewal of our mind comes about through the help and intervention, the inspiration and instruction of the Holy Spirit. And this work of the Spirit will be both direct and through the Scriptures into which he has breathed divine inspiration. There are two equal and opposite extremes that will fail to keep hold of the biblical balance of Paul's prayer. On the one hand, some Christians are keen on loving God with their minds, but they are instinctively wary, or even suspicious of, the Holy Spirit. They would be much more comfortable if God could be kept within the confines of their own reasoning. This kind of church can become like an academic seminar, very good at talking about God, with no expectation that he will ever put in a personal appearance. On the other hand, some Christians are keen on spontaneous revelation, but are instinctively wary, or even suspicious of, the human mind. They would be much more comfortable if God could be kept well away from the little grey cells. This kind of church can become like a wild west saloon, but instead of hanging up your gun at the door, you might as well hand in your brain, because all intelligent faculties will be suspended for the duration of the service. One group warns about the dangers of emotionalism, the other berates mere head knowledge. And both extremes are doomed to produce Christians who are less than fully biblical.

Paul's deliberate integration of mind and Spirit is crucial for our spiritual health and maturity as disciples. The spiritual wholeness that comes with a renewed mind is simply not possible unless we are open to the Spirit and willing to do some thoughtful Bible study and learn to love God with our minds. Christian books and teaching tapes are tremendous resources to help us in this personal growth.

At a recent conference about future technologies, speculation was growing about computer implants in the human brain. This began as a way of enabling people who are severely physically disabled to work with a computer. The interface is no longer a keyboard and mouse but a silicon implant in the brain. It sounds alarming, but it really works. This is leading to speculation that maybe one day we'll all have one. A teacher might start a lesson with the words, 'Now, children, please log on to the class computer. Today we are going to download the complete history of France.' Such technology would certainly do away with factual revision – the details would all be stored on an internal hard drive. But hackers would no doubt eagerly seize the new challenge of attempting to introduce the first computer virus to the human brain.

Whether or not such technology may emerge, one thing is clear: when I became a Christian I did not download a complete supply of spiritual wisdom. The renewal of the mind has never been instantaneous or automatic. It takes time. Psalm 119 speaks of storing up God's Word. Many Christians experience God speaking to them through the Bible day by day, with some insight and revelation of immediate relevance. And that's a wonderful privilege. But 'storing up' God's Word indicates the possibility of a longer-term investment. As we get to know the Bible, we are likely to read many things that are not immediately relevant. The more biblical insights we store up, the better equipped we are when new circumstances, opportunities or difficulties arise. The renewal of the mind is a continuing process of development, not a one-off experience.

When I was a teenager I became the proud owner of a second-hand guitar, price £1.50. I don't know whether it was the age of the guitar or the way I thrashed it, but the strings were always going out of tune. Likewise, the spiritual renewal of our mind is faced with pressures that make us keep sliding out of tune with the ways of Christ. The values of our favourite TV and radio programmes, our magazines or newspaper, conversation and priorities at work and home, even our experiences of church where fellowship can degenerate into backbiting, party spirit and gossip – in countless ways we face a daily barrage of expectations and distractions that have little to do with godly wisdom and understanding. The renewal of our mind is therefore not just about growth and progress, but it also requires recovery and self-appraisal: am I seeing life increasingly from a godly and biblical perspective, or am I getting squeezed into conformity with the way everyone else tends to approach life today? The first resource that Paul identifies for effective Christian discipleship is a renewed mind, in which our thinking is shaped and reconstructed by the Word and the Spirit.

A fruitful life

Paul's second key to effective discipleship is 'a life worthy of the Lord' (Col. 1:10). This is one of Paul's favourite phrases (1 Thess. 2:12; Phil. 1:27; Rom. 16:2; Eph. 4:1). It cannot possibly mean a life worthy of earning salvation, since Paul expressly teaches that we cannot possibly save ourselves. Salvation is a free gift of the grace of God, paid for by the crucifixion of Christ. We are saved by grace, through faith, not by works, so no Christian has any reason to boast (Eph. 2:8–9). A life worthy of the Lord is therefore the kind of life we live after we have been saved rather than a life in which we try to win God's favour by our own merit. It is a life of grateful response to the grace of Christ. A life that says thank you for the cross.

Most homes in Britain today have a video recorder. The latest models come with sophisticated and complex programmable functions. You can pre-plan a week's recordings, different channels and different times on different days. However, most people don't have a clue how to use these functions. Instead, in many homes, we simply press the record button and leave it at that. If someone is going out and the programme they want to watch starts an hour later, they press the record button right away – 'There's plenty of tape left, so I'll still catch the programme I want.' There is a generation who has completely mastered video programming, and its average age is ten. It's not that these youngsters read the manuals – they just keep pushing buttons until the machine becomes compliant with their wishes. It seems to me that an electrical retailer could make a killing if they advertised that every video player came with a free ten-year-old for the first week, to teach us how to use it properly.

Despite their electronic sophistication, most of our video recorders are used in a very basic way. They fail to live up to their potential. Similarly, when Paul prays that we may live a life worthy of the Lord, he is praying that we will fulfil our potential in Christ. As I travel the country speaking at national conferences and local events, I often meet people who tell me that there is a lot of potential in their church. This is infinitely more encouraging than if people told me that there was *no* potential in their church, but all this talk about *potential* makes me nervous. It's great to have potential, but what ultimately matters is that our potential is fulfilled. I am absolutely determined not to have as my epitaph the words 'He had some potential' – never did anything with it, but there was some sort of potential in there somewhere!

Too many people get stuck in a rut, allowing life's opportunities to pass them by. And it happens to Christians too. I can't serve God now, I don't have the experience. I would serve God now, but I need to get established in my career. I would serve God now, but I'm settling into marriage. I've got young children. I've got teen-agers. I've got so many responsibilities at work. I just don't have the energy I used to have. I prefer leaving active service to the younger generations. Before we notice, life has slipped through our fingers and we never did get to fulfil our potential in Christ.

Paul explains that as we live a worthy life we can please God in every way (Col. 1:10). This reminds us that the New Testament is more concerned about Monday morning than Sunday morning.

When someone treads on our toe at church it may be, 'Bless you, my toe seems to have got under your foot.' On Monday morning, feeling grumpy, without any other Christians around when our toe is suddenly trampled, we face a much more searching test of character. A worthy life 'in every way' speaks of whole-life discipleship and of integration: the pieces need to fit in terms of how we live at church, at home, at work and at leisure. Holiness and wholeness are both gifts of Christ to his disciples.

Paul's emphasis on *pleasing* God may come as a bit of a shock. In some churches so much emphasis is placed on our status as undeserving sinners that we come to assume that God, who is not fooled by outward piety but searches the secret motives of the heart, can only look upon us disapprovingly. God's attitude towards us seems similar to the teacher who always wrote the same phrase on our school reports: 'Could do better'. We feel that coming into God's presence is like entering the study of a severe head teacher, who only summons pupils for punishment, never for praise.

The first time I took a camera with a zoom lens to a school sports day at which one of my sons was competing, I had a wonderful time. One of his races was the 4×100 metres, and he was running the leg on the far side of the track from the parents' enclosure. Even before the race started, I was taking his picture. Before the baton got to him, and then during his leg, my shutter continued to click regularly. Once his leg was over, I continued to take his picture, until I suddenly realised that the race was over and I had forgotten to look up and see which team won. Quite without warning I had suddenly turned into Spike, the older bulldog from *Tom and Jerry* cartoons – 'That's my boy!'

Paul assures us that we really can please our Father in heaven in every way. Just as he looked upon Jesus at his baptism and declared his approval – 'This is my beloved Son, in whom I am well pleased' – he can also look upon us and declare his pleasure as we fulfil our potential in Christ – 'That's my boy! That's my girl!'

Paul adds another telling detail to this prayer about pleasing God in every way – 'bearing fruit in every good work' (Col. 1:10). Fruit has a double significance in the New Testament: it can mean the fruit of the Spirit (Gal. 5:22–3) – that is, growth in Christian character; and it can mean the fruit of witness (John 15:8) – that is, more people becoming Christians. Fruit speaks of the growth processes of the natural world: good fruit takes time to develop, and each year the harvest can become bigger and better. This underlines the fact that we are called to a living faith in which we are able to keep on making progress. If you have recently become a Christian, there is much opportunity for growth in your life. If you have been a Christian for many years, take heart, God still has much new fruit to bring into your life. However long we have been a Christian, our task is the same: to seek to please God in every way and to be determined to do all we can to fulfil our potential in Christ.

Inner strength

Paul's third concern is that we know God's inner strength. We will never make much progress in whole-life discipleship if we depend merely upon our own enthusiasm, will power or determination. Effective Christian living is only possible inasmuch as we continue to be dependent upon the Holy Spirit. The immensity of the spiritual resources available in Christ is emphasised by two phrases: 'strengthened with all power' and 'his glorious might'. Paul is not wasting words in this apparent duplication. Rather, he is attempting to convey that God's power exceeds the limits of human resources. It was the power of God that brought creation into being and the same power that raised Christ from the dead. Jesus himself promised his followers 'power from on high': they had to wait for the gift of the Spirit before attempting to fulfil the Great Commission because the Spirit is God's indispensable resource for fruitful mission.

Even so, Paul prays that we would be strengthened with this supernatural power. He clearly did not expect any of the Colossians to take offence at such a prayer: 'Paul, you're surely not suggesting that we don't have the Holy Spirit already?' Such objections miss the point entirely. Since God's power is infinite and God's love is infinite, we always have more to receive than we have known thus far. Even when we have received mightily of the Holy Spirit, we need to keep coming back for more, since the New Testament command is not to be filled with the Spirit once and then turn to other things. That would be a travesty of New Testament discipleship, for we are commanded to be filled and to go on being filled with the Holy Spirit (Eph. 5:18). (You can read much more about the Holy Spirit in a book I have written that explains his person and work – *Alive in the Spirit*, published by Hodder & Stoughton).

There are two extremist teachings about the Holy Spirit that we need to avoid. First, there are those who claim that they have no need of receiving any more of the Spirit, since they received him at conversion. However, unless their lives continually manifest the fullness of God, there is little credibility to such claims, and they need to find a new humility before God. At the opposite extreme, there are those who suggest that the power of God will lead inevitably to the victorious Church, triumphant living, unhindered advance, and unbridled happiness every day. They seem to suggest that if we can plug in properly to the power, the rest of life will be like coasting effortlessly downhill – preferably in a Ferrari. Paul's emphasis could not be more different. To the Philippians Paul affirmed that he certainly wanted to know Christ in the 'power of his resurrection'. But at the same time he was willing to embrace 'the fellowship of sharing in his sufferings' (Phil. 3:10). In fact, he was experiencing precisely this kind of fellowship, since he wrote this letter from prison, facing the prospect of imminent martyrdom.

When Paul prays for us to be strengthened with power, that's a reminder that we cannot do without the Holy Spirit for effective Christian living. Then Paul explains two particular ways in which we benefit from the Spirit's empowering presence – 'so that you may have great endurance and patience' (Col. 1:11). Endurance means putting up with difficult circumstances. Patience means putting up with difficult people. Paul recognises that we are all very likely to go through seasons of life where circumstances or people become very difficult indeed.

Here is a faith that works in the realities of daily life. In the demands of our workplace (which naturally includes the home), and equally in a time of unemployment, we can be strengthened by the Holy Spirit. In the demands of dependants, young and old, sick and needy, cantankerous and argumentative, the same strengthening of the Holy Spirit can keep us serving and loving.

Whether we face opposition for being a Christian, temptation with which we are struggling, an illness or disability that drains our resources, or aches and pains each morning that give us a stark reminder of our own mortality, in every hardship of life the Spirit is able to give us strength for living. We can sometimes slip into thinking that the Holy Spirit is reserved for God's superstars, and we create a myth of God's spiritual cavalry who go through life without a care or struggle sorting out everyone else's problems. I cannot see any such people among the Christians in the New Testament. When life gets tough, as it surely will for most of us at some time, the Holy Spirit is wonderfully available to give us the strength to keep going. He provides the vital stickability for discipleship that lasts.

Overflowing thankfulness

Paul turns quickly from this emphasis on strength in the tough times to encourage us to cultivate joyful thankfulness. Here is no stoicism without joy, gritting your teeth and grinding out a burdensome existence. Nor does Paul promote fair-weather joy, which fills our sails until the first storms come and then is seen no more. Nor a joyful unreality, in which we pretend we never have any problems at all. Far better is what Paul commends – namely, joyful thanksgiving combined with endurance and patience. That means realism, not escapism, as we face our problems squarely, but we look beyond our present needs to all that we have in Christ. God's power comes to us not for an easy ride, but to provide strength both to help us survive the tough times and to lift our hearts in joyful thanksgiving.

The first time we took our children to the Lake District, they were very young and extremely excited. When we began the ascent of Skiddaw, their initial enthusiasm suggested it was actually Everest we were about to conquer. Part way up they looked up into the clouds and pointed to the highest visible peak. 'Are we really going to climb that high?' I knew from the map that they were looking at Skiddaw Little Man, a modest pimple on the side of Skiddaw. I knew at once that if I told them we were planning to go much higher they would immediately demand a hasty retreat to the valley for an ice cream! By the time we were level with Little Man, the real Skiddaw loomed before us. What had previously filled our horizon was now a minor feature in a much larger scene. Even so, when our problems fill our horizon they can begin to consume and overwhelm us. But when we accept the discipline of giving thanks to the Father, our sights are lifted to a new horizon. The problems remain, but now they have a new setting within the wider horizon of all that we have been given in Christ.

Paul returns to this theme later in the letter, when he encourages the Colossians to be 'overflowing with thankfulness' (Col. 2:7). I remember vividly the first time I made my parents a cup of tea. In those days the custom was for children to make tea for their parents – nowadays it seems more common for parents to make mugs of coffee for their children. I poured insufficiently heated water over an inadequate quantity of tea leaves – yes, this was in the days before tea bags – and then poured out the slightly off-colour water without delay. The liquid may have been unpalatable, but the quantity was generous, since I filled those cups to the brim. By the time I had negotiated the journey from kitchen to lounge it was difficult to tell whether more tea was in the cups or the saucers. I don't remember whether my parents attempted to drink the vile brew, although I do remember them thanking me for it. One thing was certain: their cups really did overflow!

When a full cup is jolted, its contents spill over the brim. In a similar way, when we are jolted in life, whatever fills us will be sure to spill out. Jesus spelt this out plainly: 'Out of the overflow of the heart the mouth speaks' (Matt. 12:34). So here is a very direct way of assessing the condition of your heart: listen to yourself speaking. If your mouth is full of complaints and grumbling, fears and anxieties, gossip and criticism, you are able to diagnose for yourself an underlying heart problem. Paul's prayer is that we might be liberated from all such negativity. As the Spirit strengthens us with all the power of the risen Christ, he not only supplies us with strength to endure but also wants to fill us with overflowing joy. We need to learn to express our thankfulness, especially if by nature we tend to find it easier to see problems than opportunities. This kind of positive speaking and grateful appreciation is guaranteed to encourage others and strengthen our effectiveness as disciples.

Paul prayed for the Colossians to be strengthened in these vital ways, and they are just as relevant and important today:

A renewed mind, shaped by the Word and the Spirit.
A life that fulfils our potential in Christ in every way,
   so that we bring pleasure to God the Father.
The strengthening of the power of God.
Stickability in the hard times.
And a grateful heart, overflowing with joyful thanksgiving.

Like a walker preparing to set out for a day in the fells, we need to check our kit bag. Have we been neglecting any of the resources that are essential for effective discipleship?

Chapter 9

Reasons to Be Thankful

Colossians 1:12–14, 21–3

IT'S ALL VERY well to be encouraged to be more thankful, but sometimes we need a fuller picture of all that we can be thankful for. At the heart of our thankfulness is the cross of Christ, and Paul develops this theme by identifying several reasons to be thankful.

The Father has qualified you (v. 12)

With our first baby on the way I decided it was time to ask my boss for a rise. I asked for more money and he agreed. I asked for a company car and he agreed to that too. 'There's just one thing,' I added, 'I haven't passed my driving test yet.' The driving test came about a month before the baby was due. This gave an added incentive to pass first time. I didn't think Claire would appreciate the prospect of telling me in between contractions on the way to hospital that it was time to change gear. Sitting in the car at the end of the test I was impatient for the result, but tried not to show it. 'Congratulations,' the examiner said, 'you have passed.' Relief swept through me, but I decided to show no reaction at all until he had finished signing the forms. I didn't want any over-exuberance to risk giving him second thoughts.

Paul makes a much more astonishing statement than any driving examiner. He doesn't declare, 'You have qualified,' but rather 'God has qualified you.' This speaks of God's decisive and complete initiative. We've not been helped on our way a little, we've been fully qualified through the power of the cross.

Our qualifications often bestow rights and status upon us. Winners of Wimbledon tennis championships, for example, become honorary life members of the Wimbledon Lawn Tennis

Club. What God has accomplished on our behalf entitles us to 'share in the inheritance of the saints'. The saints are God's holy ones, set apart for his service. Just as God is love, his saints are called to fulfil the biblical love commands, loving God with our whole being, loving our neighbours as ourselves, and loving our fellow disciples even as Christ has loved us. Paul doesn't call us to climb Mount Holiness, in order to have sainthood conferred when we reach the summit. On the contrary, he declares that the status of sainthood is conferred freely upon us. By faith in Christ we are clothed in his righteousness, secure in his standing before the Father, and qualified among the saints of God.

A classic scene in many novels and films comes after a funeral, when a family gathers for the reading of the will. Everyone is eager to discover their portion of the inheritance. The lawyer is often interrupted by an unknown figure who sits at the back, unrecognised and unwelcome. Then, to everyone's astonishment, the will declares that the stranger has been left everything. Indignation rises in the family: 'But he's not one of us!' When God qualifies you as a holy one, he also establishes you as a rightful heir. In the Roman world, once you had adopted a child they had the full and irrevocable rights of your blood children. They were yours for always. Similarly, by faith in Christ we have been adopted into God's eternal family. And God has no favourites: he loves every one of his children with equal generosity and kindness.

In the present there is no need for anyone to feel like a second-class Christian. And there's no need to worry that in the future you may miss out on heaven. You can afford to be confident, not because of pride and arrogance, but because the Father has qualified you. That's Paul's first reason to be thankful.

The Father has rescued us (v. 13)

A few years ago we went on holiday to Cornwall. The first evening was glorious. We found a hidden cove, reached only through a cave at low tide. The sand was clean, and the sea sparkled under the evening sun. It was a foretaste of paradise.

The next morning it began to rain, and the rain continued for a fortnight. All over Cornwall and Devon parents were running out of ideas to keep young children entertained and running out of money to pay for it! One evening we came back to the small harbour village where we were staying and there was a rescue helicopter hovering over the cliffs. Soon the harbour area was packed with children who had rushed out to see the free show. We learnt that a young lad had clambered down the cliffs during the afternoon, looking for more exciting places to explore. At first it was wonderful fun, but eventually he was faced with a sheer drop to the sea and could go no further. Only then did he realise that climbing up was going to prove a lot harder than clambering down. It was impossible for him to get himself off the cliffs, but he was still in good voice and soon attracted the attention of a family who called for Air-Sea Rescue to come and do their stuff.

Paul lent the weight of his apostolic ministry to the assertion that the Colossians really had joined the company of God's saints – 'God has qualified *you*.' Now he shifts to the first person: 'The Father has rescued *us*.' Paul insists that he needed rescuing as much as anyone else. All of us were in trouble and have been thrown the same lifeline of salvation thanks to the cross of Christ.

God's rescue operation loosens us from 'the dominion of darkness', that is, the grip of Satan and the rule of selfish living. An obvious parallel is Europe in the grip of Hitler, when courageous individuals sought to rescue Jews or prisoners of war. Just as such rescuers were willing to risk their own lives, God was prepared to sacrifice his eternally beloved Son for the sake of the lost.

Earlier in the day, the boy on the cliff in Cornwall would not have welcomed the attention of the helicopter and the rescue team. He would have seen them as intruding on his fun without good reason. However, once he realised that he was trapped, their arrival brought relief, gratefulness, and even tears of joy. Similarly, the good news of the gospel is not really good news until we have seen that we need it. Only when we realise that we are in the grip of selfishness and in desperate need of forgiveness does the cross of Christ become truly welcome. We have to grasp the bad news of an entrapment from which we cannot save ourselves before we can fully appreciate the good news that we can be rescued by faith in Christ. God's rescue plan is Paul's second reason to be grateful.

The Father has brought us into his kingdom (v. 13)

The greatest event in the history of the Jews up to the birth of Christ was the Exodus, when Moses led the people out of bondage in Egypt towards freedom in the Promised Land. This decisive rescue operation of the Old Testament is recalled in this promise of entry to the kingdom of God. There are no half measures in God's plan of salvation. We are not rescued from our past, forgiven our sin, brought back to ground zero, and given a second chance in life, only to be left to our own devices. The rescue is complete and the contrast is absolute. The previous existence, paralleling slavery in Egypt, was bondage in the dominion of darkness. The new life, paralleling freedom and the Promised Land, brings wonderful new opportunities to our lives.

Paul describes the new kingdom in two ways. It is the 'kingdom of light', in contrast to the 'dominion of darkness'. That speaks of purity, vibrancy, wholeness and abundant life. It is also the 'kingdom of the Son he loves'. This emphasises that the Son of God is the King of the kingdom, and when the Father brings us into his kingdom we come under the rule of his Son. The Son who is King is deeply loved by the Father, which emphasises that this is the kingdom of everlasting love. The dominion of darkness is centred upon power, control, exploitation and selfishness. The kingdom of light is centred upon love, freedom, bringing out the best in others, and servanthood. This transfer between kingdoms is Paul's third reason to be grateful.

These great saving acts of God are secured in the cross of Christ. Paul makes this plain in the phrase 'in whom we have' (v. 14). The Father's saving purposes, to qualify, rescue and transfer us into the kingdom, are all fulfilled and completed at the cross. The power of the cross is further reinforced by two additional aspects that Paul briefly highlights.

Redemption at the Cross (v. 14)

In the cross we have 'redemption'. That means liberation, recalling Israel's rescue from Egyptian slavery. Today the word 'redeem' is used mainly in the context of pawnbrokers: you pay the required price to buy back an item previously deposited in the shop. In the

Roman Empire, a slave could be redeemed on payment of a required price. Christ's substitutionary death secures our freedom, paying the price that can bring us liberation once for all.

Forgiveness at the Cross (v. 14)

In the cross we also have 'forgiveness'. This is forgiveness bought at a price. In the Old Testament, the sacrificial system symbolised the price of forgiveness. An animal was killed and the sinner was forgiven. In the New Testament, the sacrificial system reaches its fulfilment at the cross. Christ is the spotless lamb of God who pays the price once for all. When he is made sin in our place, by his atoning sacrifice we can secure everlasting forgiveness from the Father and our sins can be separated from us for ever.

For many years Heineken ran adverts jokily claiming that their lager could refresh the parts no other beer could reach. Out of this campaign developed a sequel, in which, even more obliquely, we were told, 'Only Heineken can do all this.' In the New Testament, God's saving actions are focused decisively and triumphantly in the cross of Christ. Redemption and forgiveness are the fourth and fifth reasons to be grateful, and the sixth is that all of this has been secured at Golgotha. Only the cross of Christ can do all this. And all of this is ours, if we have put our trust in him.

Alienated and reconciled (vv. 21–3)

Later in chapter 1 of Colossians Paul returns to the theme of all that has been accomplished at the cross, and we can identify still more reasons to be thankful. Once again there is bad news to face before the good news can be fully appreciated, and Paul describes us as previously alienated from God. One of my least welcome sights at any airport is the word with which Americans welcome foreigners: 'Aliens'. It makes it sound as if we have green skin and will be making a special guest appearance on the *X-Files*. The hardest country to get into and out of, at least for me, has always been Israel. Maybe I have the facial characteristics or behaviour patterns that are typical of an international terrorist. I am invariably searched and interrogated at length, while whoever is travelling with me has to patiently wait on the other side of the barrier. Israeli passport control invariably gives me a very strong experience of alienation, of being an outsider.

Paul explains that the human race has become alienated from God – that is, cut off, isolated, and suffering the consequences of a broken relationship. What's more, we are enemies of God in our minds. Paul's harsh language confirms that the human race has developed a bias against God and godliness. Just as our thinking reveals our alienation from God, it is also demonstrated in behaviour that Paul calls 'evil'. In our attitudes and values we have torn up the love commands of the Bible, living selfishly towards others and without any reference to God. Paul is suggesting that evil behaviour characterises not merely a Stalin, Hitler or Pol Pot, but every single human being on the face of the earth. Alongside this bias to selfishness is a self-justifying attitude. The human instinct is to try to save ourselves and demonstrate our presumed worthiness of salvation by showing how much better we are than others. But the good news of the gospel is for those who cannot save themselves. There is no salvation without facing the need for salvation. Conversion is only good news for those who have realised that they are sinners. The old spiritual got it exactly right: 'It's not my brother nor my sister but it's me, O Lord, standing in the need of prayer.'

Paul declares confidently that God has reconciled us through Christ's physical body. When I was an undergraduate, one evangelist visiting the Christian Union (actually, it was David Watson) preached about Jesus as the only and perfect bridge between us and God. He can be the bridge because he was fully God and fully man, the Son of God incarnate. And he became that bridge by dying in our place. A friend of mine, Helen, listened carefully to David. It seemed to make sense, but something more was needed to clinch things for her. She went back to her room to think some more, and as she sat there she started gazing at a poster that her room-mate, a Christian student called Kate, had just put up. At the middle of the picture was a beautiful bridge. Suddenly Helen knew that she simply had to cross that bridge, by faith in Christ, and be reconciled to the Father.

Reconciliation speaks of restored relationship. The rift is healed. What had been broken is mended. This new standing is described by Paul in three ways: holy in his sight, free from accusation, and without blemish. Holy in his sight is the natural standing of the Son before the Father. From all eternity their relationship knew only purity and love. His life on earth saw no end to this perfection: when he challenged his opponents to name one act of selfishness in his life, they were unable to point to anything. But how can we be holy in God's sight when Paul has only just described us as God's enemies? The answer of course is the great exchange of the cross. The crucifixion of Christ is a kind of cosmic swap shop, where he takes upon himself our sinfulness and its due penalty, so that we can receive in its place his right standing before the Father and the favour that is his due. 'God made him who had no sin to be sin for us, so that in him we might become the righteousness of God' (2 Cor. 5:21).

Peter and Jenny were much better at spending money than keeping hold of it. They kept taking out more credit cards, using them to pay one another off, and so their debts kept rising at an alarming rate. Eventually they got a grip on the problem, took some financial advice, destroyed most of their credit cards, and worked to settle their debts as quickly as possible. There was great joy when they finally received a statement that confirmed that there were no more debts outstanding. Everything had been paid in full. Likewise, Paul says that we can be 'free from accusation'. Not because our lives have been absolutely blameless, but because of the reconciling power of the cross. Christ took the blame, so that we might know the Father's love.

Our lives in Christ are also 'without blemish'. I enjoy watching the *Antiques Roadshow* from time to time. If it were filmed in the States, I could imagine people whooping with excitement as they discover their treasured possession really is an incredibly expensive antique. Because it's filmed in Britain by the BBC, everyone is terribly restrained. 'I should get it insured for £10,000,' the expert advises. The proud owner nods her head cautiously and observes, 'How interesting.' The next guest has brought in something even more wonderful. It would have been worth £25,000,' the expert concludes, 'but this crack reduces its value to around £2,000.' Once again, because this is a British programme, the response is restrained, 'How interesting.' We never do discover what sanctions are imposed upon the child whose indoor football game produced the crack, nor whether the owner has quite such a stiff upper lip once the cameras are no longer running. To be without blemish means that God considers us to be in mint condition. No running repairs on our lives could convince even the most casual observer that our lives have no blemishes at all. But God is the master restorer. The grime of the years, when we have been sinned against and sinning, can be completely stripped away by the restorative power of the cross.

Here, then, is a glorious sequence of reasons to be thankful:

> We have been qualified.
> We have been rescued.
> We have been transferred.
> We have been redeemed.
> We have been forgiven.
> We have been reconciled.
> We have been made holy in his sight.
> We have been granted freedom from accusation.
> We have been restored without blemish.

All of this has been accomplished through the saving power of the death of Christ on our behalf. Only the cross of Christ can do all this, and so there are very good reasons indeed for us to overflow with grateful thanksgiving.

Staying with the gospel

Paul concludes this section by adding a conditional clause. All of these reasons to be thankful apply in our lives, so long as we continue in our faith. We not only need to enter into personal saving faith, we also need to stick with it, 'not moved from the hope held out in the gospel' (Col. 1:23).

I read my first degree at the University of York, where the campus is built around a lake that often freezes in winter. Late one December evening I was walking back to my room when I saw a drunken student trying to test the ice before embarking on some night-time skating. He stood on the bank stamping furiously with one foot on ice that seemed solid and secure. Without warning, the ice suddenly gave way, just as he had placed more weight on his testing foot than the foot on dry ground. He toppled quickly into the icy water, quite incapable of doing anything to prevent his imminent soaking. I have never seen someone sober up so quickly.

When Paul urges us not to move from the hope of the gospel, he is urging us to have both feet planted firmly in gospel truth. There should be no hedging of our bets, no half and half, no double life when we are out of sight of other believers, no semi-commitment. If the Apache or Sioux didn't have this saying, they should have: he who rides two horses ends up by falling off both. Paul invites us to examine ourselves and make certain that we are leaning on Christ with all our weight. We need to depend on him fully, both feet on solid rock.

And so we end this chapter with a very practical question. Where are you in your commitment to Christ? Maybe you have never come to living faith. If so, you are still in need of rescue, forgiveness and reconciliation, and I urge you to make the decision to come to Christ in faith and begin a new life. Maybe you have one foot in the faith. If so, I urge you to come over completely to the service of Christ. Maybe you are a wholehearted believer. If so, I encourage you to enjoy your standing in Christ. In him is a security that cannot be shattered, a hope that will remain true for all eternity, a love that is immense, free and totally reliable for all who put their trust in him. No half measures make sense. I urge you to choose and continue to choose the fulfilling path of whole-life discipleship.

Chapter 10

Your Christ Is Too Small

Colossians 1:15–17

COSMOPOLITAN MAGAZINE RECENTLY announced a 'Virtual Make-over for Women' CD-ROM. Users scan in a personal photo and ask the computer to experiment with new hair, new make-up, a new wardrobe, or even a new figure enhanced by plastic surgery. In a few seconds an exact representation of a new you appears on the screen. If a similar CD was made available for men of a certain age, I suspect it would only need two option buttons: more on top and less round the middle.

An essential principle of the Old Testament is that the Lord God is invisible, transcendent and mysterious. The second commandment provided strict instructions that the Jews should not try to represent God in pictorial form, because in his majesty God is beyond the limits of the human imagination. Rather than depending on our attempts to construct an artistic image, he is the God who reveals himself through both his actions and his words.

Towards the end of Jesus' ministry, Philip voiced a frustration that the other disciples may have shared. Jesus kept emphasising that we can know God as Father, but his followers wanted something more. 'Lord, show us the Father,' Philip requested, 'and that will be enough for us.' Jesus' response is immediate: 'Anyone who has seen me has seen the Father' (John 14:8–9). If we want to know the character of the Father, we need look no further than the person of the Son. Paul takes up the same theme: 'He is the image of the invisible God' (Col. 1:15). This does not suggest that Jesus provides us with a good likeness, a degree of similarity, or some kind of imitation of God. Paul declares he is the *ikon* of God, which means the exact representation, the revelation of the invisible. He is God's ultimate, unique, definitive self-revelation. In Jesus' teaching, his character and his essential being, God makes himself known.

If we want to know what God is really like, we need to begin not with our own ideas or experiences, bad or good, but with Jesus. Similarly, if we want to interpret the Old Testament properly, which looks forward to Jesus, and the New Testament, which looks back to Jesus, our study of the Scriptures needs to be Jesus centred. He is God's most authoritative Word about himself.

Paul explains how the Jesus of history can accomplish this definitive revelation by explaining the eternal origins of the Son of God: 'the firstborn over all creation' (Col. 1:15). 'Firstborn' speaks of sonship, the intimate relationship between Father and child. 'Over all creation' makes a vital distinction between the Son and creation and also emphasises his Lordship. He is not the firstborn *of* creation, which would establish the Son as the first created being. Rather he is *over* creation, which underlines his uniqueness. Before the creation comes into being, the Son already is. And once creation comes about, he is 'over all', that is, Lord of all created beings. Just like John in the prologue to his Gospel (John 1:1–2), Paul is teaching the pre-existence of the Son. While his human flesh had a specific beginning in space and time, within Mary's womb, his divine nature is eternal and existed with the Father and the Spirit before the dawn of time and the birth of creation.

What follows is a magnificent hymn of the cosmic Christ. We cannot be sure whether Paul wrote it or is quoting from an existing early Christian poem. The hymn develops a celebration of the twofold Lordship of Christ. He is Lord of the Church, which is a familiar notion to every Christian today, and he is also Lord of the cosmos. If we only think of Christ in terms of the historical life of Jesus of Nazareth, and if we only think of his Lordship in terms of the Church and the religious sphere of life, we have completely missed the point. Paul explores the Lordship of Christ over the Church and the cosmos in three similar ways: he is their source, their head and their sustainer. First, his relationship with the cosmos is celebrated.

Lord of the cosmos

1 *Christ is the source of creation* – 'by him all things were created' (Col. 1:16). The totality of the cosmos' dependence upon the Son is emphasised by repetition. Without exception, all things material and spiritual owe their existence to the Son. This means every kind of angelic being is dependent upon Christ, which rules out any possibility of an equal and opposite force of evil, and also excludes the notions with which the Colossians had begun to toy of some kind of intermediate spirits between God and the creation of the material world. As the source of creation, the Son is the one who puts into action the loving and creative purposes of the Father.

2 *Christ is the head of creation*, because all was created 'for him' (Col. 1:16). This means that creation has been fashioned for Christ's glory, declaring the wonder of his cosmic artistry and ordering. It was also brought into being for his pleasure and delight, expressive of his character, and ultimately accountable to him. Christ, not humankind, is the centre of creation. There is more beauty, variety and splendour in the natural world than any human being can ever fully appreciate. What's more, some parts of creation are of no benefit to us, but bring glory and pleasure to the Son. Above all, creation is not ultimately designed for our profit-centred, short-term exploitation: the circle of life owes its ultimate allegiance not to us but to the Son of God.

3 *Christ is the sustainer of creation*. He was before all things as the Creator at the dawn of time, but Christ also stays involved for 'in him all things hold together' (Col. 1:17). God is not like a traditional watchmaker who completes his precision timepiece, winds it up, and then leaves it to run by itself. The Creator keeps his creation going, preserving the harmonies of the cosmos, and renewing the gift of life. Anyone with a garden will know that it takes effort to keep it under control. How much more complex, beyond the limits of human imagining, is the continuing task of the Lord of creation as he keeps the entire cosmos in perfect harmony.

This majestic concept of the Lordship of Christ gives meaning and purpose to the cosmos. The one who has revealed the character of the Father is the one who gives creative order and vitality to the natural world. This has many wonderful implications for the

Christian disciple, giving the themes of Genesis 1–3 an extra dimension of personal responsibility.

First, Christ's Lordship of the cosmos underlines our ecological responsibility. When the pavements and parks are covered in litter and the atmosphere is burdened with lead deposits and acid rain, the disfigurement of creation is a dishonour to the Son of God. In our care for creation, we express our worship of Christ. Recycling waste products, avoiding non-recyclable products, and discouraging wasteful use of cars without passengers are all fitting responsibilities for the disciples of the Lord of creation.

Second, Christ the Creator gives encouragement to our creativity, whether through admiring the beauty of creation and the artistry of others, or through expressing our own artistry – in painting or poetry, photography or pottery, dance or mime, playing or composing music, gardening or interior decoration, designing a website, or some other art form. Many of us struggle to get back in touch with our creativity, living in a world that has set little value by these kinds of personal expression. We need to recover the wonderful truth that we can take pleasure in artistry to the honour of Christ, the ultimate master craftsman.

Third, the Lordship of Christ encourages scientific exploration as an expression of our whole-life discipleship. Since creation is shaped by the mind of Christ, we discover something more of the character of Christ as we unveil the mysteries of the created order. Christian faith promotes scientific enquiry with nothing to fear from discoveries in the laboratory. Science is an invaluable field of human endeavour and operates best within an agreed ethical framework because Christ is the Lord of creation.

Not just in the religious sphere but in the totality of life, Christ is the Cosmic Lord. Whatever we enjoy in life, we can appreciate all the more when we realise we are taking delight in the wonderfully good gifts of the Son of God. The superabundant splendours of creation express the infinite artistry and generosity of the eternal Son of God. A generation ago, J. B. Phillips, a great Bible translator, wrote a book called *Your God Is Too Small*. We can summarise this hymn of the cosmic Christ with a similar phrase – your Christ is too small.

Lord of the Church

In the first section of this great hymn, Christ is the source, head and sustainer of creation (Col. 1:15–17). In the second section, he is presented as the source, head and sustainer of the Church (Col. 1:17–20). Christ's Lordship of the Church is vital to grasp, since we have often ignored it to our great discredit. Some years ago I was working with some others one Saturday morning at a town centre church. The building had a narrow forecourt that was used for very limited parking in a single line. Because of the risk of cars blocking one another for hours at a time, a sign had been put up explaining that car parking was restricted to those who were using the church premises.

Suddenly the doors of the building flew open and a woman erupted into the building. 'Someone,' she protested, 'has blocked me in.' We expressed our regret and explained that this was always a risk with the inadequate car parking arrangements, which is why the sign stated that car parking was restricted to those using the building. 'But I'm a church member!' she expostulated. She wasn't a member of that particular church, but of some church somewhere. It was not until that moment that I discovered that church membership entitled you to free car parking at any church premises in the country!

1 *Christ is the source of the Church*, the beginning and the firstborn from among the dead (Col. 1:18). Sometimes when I visit churches, people point out to me their surviving 'founder members'. Other churches have their walls festooned with brass plaques commemorating those who have advanced the church through their generous donations of time, money or equipment. My own view is that the sooner we do away with such memorials the better. It would come as no surprise to me if one day we hear of a church building that has collapsed under the weight of the brass plaques. No business or retail outlet would clutter its main public space with such things. Instead of releasing the church for the future, such plaques shackle our buildings to the past, making them look like memorials for previous eras rather than premises to serve the needs of today's rising generations.

I have come across at least two churches that have plaques commemorating the gift of a sound system when the equipment has since been replaced more than once. Many churches dare not shift inconvenient furnishings for fear of offending the relatives of the original donor. In one church I visited there was a huge communion table, quite out of proportion to the rest of the building. 'We can't move it,' someone explained, 'It was given in memory of a founder member and his son is still in the church.' The son was about eighty-five, and so I had a quick word to ask what he thought about the table. 'Horrible thing,' he said, 'I can't imagine why they didn't get rid of it years ago.'

There's a similar problem in some churches with rugs and easy chairs: when people have no more use for them at home, they give them to the church with the unintended result that they clutter up the premises for years. For fear of offending one another, we turn our buildings into mausoleums. It should be a precondition of any gift that the church has the right to use it for as long as it wants and to dispose of it in whatever way seems appropriate. As to taking offence, the gospel of grace is contradicted every time a Christian gets sulky or spiky or grizzles that they have been hard done by. All Christian disciples should take a vow of abstinence from being easily offended. We need to learn to be difficult to upset, slow to anger, and quick to forgive.

Christ is the 'beginning' because the Church starts with his death and resurrection. His atoning sacrifice makes the new creation possible. He is the 'firstborn' because he is the first to receive a resurrection body. Just as he preceded the cosmos and brought it into being, he does the same for his Church. As a result, since he is the only originator, the only founder member, in everything he has supremacy: his pre-eminence is unassailable. There is no contest, no rivals. The risen Christ has no need for any helpers in starting the Church, neither Mary and the saints, nor priests, nor apostles, nor anointed leaders, nor major donors. Christ accomplished all that was required for his Church to be born. He is all that we need and he deserves all the glory. If there must be a brass plaque in a church, perhaps it should read something like this:

This building is dedicated to the glory of Jesus Christ,
the only and all-sufficient founder member of his church.

Soli Deo gloriae

2 *Christ is the head of his Church* (Col. 1:18). Because the Church is the body and Christ is the head, this speaks of his authority and his glory. His authority, because we are under his command. His glory, because our priority is not to bring attention to ourselves, but to our Master. I have met many people who speak about 'my church' in a way that is potentially dangerous. It's a question of ownership. If we feel that we belong to our church, and we gladly accept that it's the risen Christ who sets the agenda for his Church, that's a very healthy combination. But if we make the shift to treating the Church like a religious club for insiders, decline is almost inevitable. I heard of one church where the farmers decided at market on Tuesday what the PCC would agree on Wednesday. In some churches it is accepted that one family runs everything: if you aren't related, you can never be a leader. Sometimes it's a minister who dominates a church in an unhealthy way. Sometimes it's a leadership team or the founder members. I have come across churches that in theory welcome growth, so long as the established circle of insiders stays in control and the newcomers understand that they are visitors who should never interfere with the existing patterns of worship and church life. Such attitudes can be summed up in a phrase that is usually a kiss of death to spiritual vitality: 'It's all very well that new people are joining the church, but what's in it for me?' A friend of mine was pastoring a church where a long-established leader told him he would rather the church die than grow and change. The warning is clear: the only healthy Lord of the Church is Christ himself, and when any of us attempts to control the Church, however honourable our initial motives, trouble is sure to follow.

There are three centres of authority for local church life, the members, the leaders and external church authorities. Different denominations work out the interaction between these three in various ways: Congregational churches emphasise the members' meeting; Presbyterian churches emphasise the leadership team; Episcopal churches emphasise the regional and national leaders of the denomination or stream. Within this broad range of choices, individual churches naturally work out their distinctive way of establishing an interaction between these different sources of authority: at best, the experience is creative and constructive; at worst, it becomes a stalemate or even destructive. I have not yet come across any kind of pattern of church government that is bomb-proof: things can go wrong in any structure. Leadership teams can become authoritarian and remote; members' meetings can become petty and give expression to party spirit; external input can become irrelevant or even dictatorial.

Whatever our pattern of church government and however we choose to have these three centres of decision-making interact, we need to ensure that the Lordship of Christ is clearly affirmed. I came across an Anglican church that held a special service in which the vicar acted out his own 'dethroning' in order to explicitly enthrone Christ as Lord of the Church. In one Baptist church, everyone knelt during a half night of prayer to affirm that their desire was not to impose their own opinions and preferences, but to seek together the mind of Christ. There is, according to the New Testament, only one Lord of the Church. If anyone else assumes full control, disappointment and frustration are sure to follow.

The Lordship of Christ is not meant to be sobering, dreary or negative. The creative power of the Lord of the cosmos, the resurrection power of the Lord of life, the extravagant grace of the Lord of the cross, all these glorious, supernatural resources belong to the Church that is yielding to Christ as Lord. In the Gospels, the first disciples often seemed to have no idea what Jesus would do next, but he was sure to find some new way of expressing the immensity of God's love. Likewise, where Christ is unreservedly given control of his Church, the ride may be unpredictable, but the outcome promises to be exceptional. Other lords of the church often lead to bad feelings and boredom, disputes and decline. It's time to give the Church back to Jesus Christ.

3 *Christ is the sustainer of his Church.* Just as he keeps the cosmos together, the creative and loving power of God keeps the Church going and ensures that it stays on track. That's why we can always afford to be optimistic about the ultimate destiny of the Church. Our confidence is not in human insights and leadership, whether through individuals or teams, synods or committees. Our confidence is in the risen Christ who sustains his Church in fulfilment of the Great Commission.

There are several strands to the sustaining power of Christ. First, he sustains by his permanent revelation. Since all the fullness of God is found in Christ (Col. 1:19), he is beyond comparison. No higher revelation is possible because Christ is God's definitive and unsurpassable self-disclosure. Therefore, whatever our circumstances, opportunities or pressures, we have a constant reference point and inspiration in the person and teaching of Jesus Christ.

Second, Christ sustains his Church by his permanent atonement. There is no sell-by date to the power of the cross. Full satisfaction has been made for every stain of sin, with no extra price to pay. Once for all, he has made peace through his blood (Col. 1:20).

Third, he sustains his Church with a permanent priority, namely reconciliation (Col. 1:22). We are called to follow in the ways of the Reconciler, communicating forgiveness, mercy and love. That means we need to demonstrate and declare the reconciling power of the cross, expressing Christ's love through actions and words in our daily lives.

Fourth, he sustains his Church with the permanence of his love. All too often the Church has been quick to sin and slow to obey. Maybe you have been personally disappointed by the Church at some time – I know I have. But I also know that I have much more often been a great disappointment to the risen Christ. We are called to love the Church because Christ continues to love his Church, and to be patient with the Church even as Christ has needed to be so very patient with each of us.

Fifth, Christ sustains his Church as his body in action, throughout the world. There are no denominations and streams in the New Testament, just local churches and the universal Church. At their best, denominations and streams are useful resource agencies for the local church. At their worst, they distract us from biblical inclusiveness. We should never despise others or be tempted to claim any kind of monopoly of the truth or the Spirit. I am always sick at heart when I hear members of any denomination or stream looking down on everyone else and writing them off as if they were sub-standard. The universal Church, sustained by Christ himself, encompasses all who own Jesus as Saviour and Lord. When we honour the universal Church, we honour her source, head and sustainer.

Lord of all

The unsurpassable glory of Christ is expressed in his all-inclusive Lordship. He is the source, the head and the sustainer of both the cosmos and the Church. This calls us to an all-encompassing faith, in which every aspect of life is brought into creative connection with Jesus Christ. This is not the way that Christians have usually lived. The medieval Church split life into two compartments, the sacred and the secular, and created two tiers of Christian: the celibate comprised the spiritual premier league, and those who were married came a poor second. Today we have developed our own distortions of whole-life discipleship. We create a compartmentalism, in which Christ is only connected to the 'spiritual' aspects of life. We create a church–centredness, a cradle-to-grave total-life experience in which no evening is complete without a church-based activity or committee. We create an other-worldly spirituality, in which life outside of church, at work and at leisure, seems often a distraction at best and a sinful indulgence at worst. Since the Lord of every believer's life is Lord of both the Church and the cosmos, we need to break free from this distorted thinking and narrow spirituality.

1 *Christ is the Lord of time*. The three pivotal moments of cosmic history are in the hands of Christ. At the dawn of time, the eternal Son brought creation into being. At just the right time, the kairos moment, the incarnate Son became the all-sufficient atoning sacrifice at the cross. And at the end of time, the ascended Son will return in glory as the judge of the living and the dead. Here is an eternal framework that gives meaning, stability and hope. Whatever uncertainties and pressures we may face from day to day, our confidence remains secure in the Lord of time.

2 *Christ is the Lord of reconciliation*. Pivotal to Christ's purposes is mending relationships and rebuilding broken lives. Reconciliation was won at the cross (Col. 1:20), and is now the continuing work of the risen Christ, together with the Father and the Spirit. In professional sport, certain players can be guaranteed to react if others get into an argument. Some will join in, fists flying. Others will intervene to pull apart those squaring up for a fight. As servants of the Lord of reconciliation, we are called to shape our lives around the priority of reconciliation, in our words, actions and prayers.

We need to be realistic: human nature means that misunderstandings, communication breakdowns and failures of relationship are likely from time to time. We also need to be defiantly hopeful: our Lord is the Cosmic Reconciler, whose passion is to take us beyond our entrenched attitudes, bitterness and hostility.

One of the saddest sights is a Christian, especially a Christian leader, who starts attacking others to protect his or her own position. At the first hint of vindictiveness, aggression and bolstering our own position by attacking others, our credibility as disciples is shot to pieces. If we cannot be fully reconciled with another Christian, because they are incapable of abandoning hostility and manipulation or are unwilling to say sorry, then we must walk the path of forgiveness, refusing to be sucked into retaliation, hostility or bitterness. If we are serious about following the Lord of reconciliation, life is too short to waste time and energy by holding grudges and indulging in negative talk. We need to learn to let go and move on in Jesus' way of love.

3 *Christ is the Lord of life*. The time each week that we spend away from other Christians, at work, at leisure and at home, is certainly not irrelevant to Christ. His loving Lordship encompasses every single aspect of life. We need to be freed from false guilt: some Christians develop a fear that if they enjoy anything it almost certainly must be wrong. Jesus was filled with love of life. The Gospels show him enjoying wine, food and laughter with friends and strangers. His first miracle supplied extra wine to help a wedding feast go well. The sights and sounds of everyday life in Galilee are found in his parables, as he tells stories about families, farming, fishing and the flowers of the field. In his resurrection body, he revealed himself to be more alive than ever, capable of entering a locked room and yet enjoying a cooked breakfast. And he promised that the new age of heaven would begin with a great wedding banquet, complete with wine. Jesus observed life keenly, lived it actively, and enjoyed it to the full.

This has thrilling implications for every Christian. At work, we can seek to live for Christ and in his presence. At leisure, we can enjoy our favourite activities in the company of Christ. For me, some of the most sublime moments in life have come about when I discovered certain great works of art for the first time: a Racine tragedy, Michelangelo's captives, Schubert's Great Symphony, Matisse's cut-outs and Puccini's *La Bohème*. Delight in whatever gives us pleasure goes up another gear when we can turn our admiration into appreciation before Christ. When you see a baby content in its mother's arms, young lovers gazing into one another's eyes, majestic mountain scenery, the delicate beauty of a single snowdrop, or an infinitude of other splendours of both creation and human artistry, Christians more than anyone else should be able to take great delight – 'What a wonderful world!' We can be rich with life, fully alive, filled with *joie de vivre*, enjoying life in all its fullness, capable of taking great delight even in the smallest pleasures of life, because we are followers of Jesus Christ, and he is the Lord of life.

Chapter 11

Serving to Lead

Colossians 1:21–9
SUCCESSFUL LEADERSHIP IS highly competitive, in sport, business and politics. People struggle to climb the greasy pole, then have to ward off others to retain their prominence. James and John were a pair of brothers among Jesus' disciples who brought familiar competitive instincts into their discipleship. Like an agent who signs up a young sporting star before others get to him, they tried to get to Jesus first, negotiating for the best seats in heaven before anyone else had noticed that there could be a deal to be made.

They began their critical conversation with Jesus by seeking an open-ended guarantee: 'We want you to do for us whatever we ask' (Mark 10:35). Jesus was far too shrewd to make such a promise, but invited them to explain what they had in mind. When they spelt out their ambitions, Jesus promptly dismissed their request. To sit on his right and left is for those duly appointed by the Father. There is no inside track or preferential seating for those who happen to lodge an early application.

When the other disciples heard about James' and John's failed request they were indignant. Sadly, it's possible that they were angry not so much because they disapproved of such a request, but because they were being bypassed by the ambitious brothers. Perhaps some wished that they had been the first to think of such an approach, or even wondered whether they stood a chance of a more favourable reply. Jesus' subsequent explanation of kingdom leadership was not reserved for James and John. Instead, Jesus decided that the entire team of disciples needed to hear about a radically new way of exercising leadership (Mark 10:42–5).

Jesus expressly forbids three things that are normal in leadership.

First, he describes the way that Gentile rulers 'lord it over' people. This speaks of domination, the heavy-handed love of power that strips people of their full human dignity and treats them as mere underlings. The Gentile approach to leadership is little more than dictatorship. It may be malevolent, concerned with maximising power for the ruler, or it may consider itself quite benign, providing others with a sense of security and order. Either way, it is unavoidably – and in Jesus' terms, unacceptably – authoritarian. Different churches are tempted to legitimise leaders who 'lord it over' the people in a variety of ways. Some explain that only the priest, ministers or those theologically trained have the expertise to exercise leadership, and everyone else must follow, without question. Others claim a monopoly of Holy Spirit anointing for the leadership team: if you are not persuaded by their approach you are failing to respond to the guidance of the Holy Spirit. Some leaders are domineering by nature, others become over-bearing out of their own insecurities which they hide behind being too pushy. Whatever the reasons, personal and denominational, whether it is a traditional church or one that's very new, Jesus' wise warning still applies: there is no room or justification for such things in the kingdom of God.

Second, Jesus acknowledges the natural human instinct to compare ourselves with one another. In particular, Jesus identifies the desire of some leaders to be considered great and to ascend to the top of the pile. Jesus doesn't entirely repudiate such motivations, but he insists that they must be taken in an entirely new and rather surprising direction. To be great and considered a winner in the kingdom of heaven is not about achievement, self-assertion or being admired for your accomplishments. On the contrary, true greatness and true leadership will be expressed, according to Jesus, in our willingness to serve others freely.

Third, Jesus spells out what we must look for in kingdom leadership. Like him, our priority must be to serve others rather than be served. One of the hardest things I did as a young Christian was to read some early church history. Not because it was boring, but because it only took a few generations for a number of Christian leaders to ignore wilfully the express teaching of Jesus. They became envious of one another, power hungry, keen on prestige and pomp, rivals of one another, and overbearing towards the people. Whenever we do such things we cannot claim with any credibility to be wholehearted followers of Jesus Christ. I was talking with a couple who host Christian conferences on a regular basis. They told me that the best of Christian leaders are a great delight, men and women keen to serve others and never wanting to make any kind of fuss. Some, however, start behaving like Hollywood prima donnas, imposing upon their entourage a litany of unreasonable complaints and impulsive demands.

The snare of power and prestige can be quite insidious. Larry served a church for many years and his motivation was excellent. Eventually, however, a new thought took root in Larry's mind: 'This church owes me something for all I've done here.' Once he felt that way, he began to make demands that would have been unthinkable in earlier years. Because the church would no longer comply with his every demand for attention and his every preference in worship, Larry grew resentful. He felt unloved and he became increasingly unlovely, more likely to complain than encourage, more likely to make demands than offer to help. The whisper of the tempter had struck a chord in Larry's heart and he changed from being a servant to a rejected master. If only he had kept hold of the wholesome attitudes of a servant heart that had characterised his earlier years of service!

When Jesus was rebuking the Pharisees, he was even more robust in rejecting the normal patterns of religious life. The rabbis, Jesus explained, loved the attention and respect that their status and title conferred. But Jesus insisted that we enjoy a remarkable equality as brothers and sisters which should exclude any emphasis upon our status. We should not call anyone by the standard names of religious life: 'teacher', 'master', 'father'. A higher authority – that is, God himself – has already claimed exclusive right to such titles. The true expression of human greatness, Jesus emphasised, is not to seize every opportunity to exalt ourselves, but rather to seek to serve at all times. According to Jesus' reversal of normal leadership standards, the 'greatest among you will be your servant' (Matt. 23:7–12). In few areas of discipleship have we been so willing to institutionalise the reverse of Jesus' teaching, since we have conferred upon church leaders so many titles that his teaching sought to exclude.

Spiritual abuse

I was so grateful to *Renewal* magazine when they approached me a couple of years ago to write an article exploring the problem of spiritual abuse. To be honest, it was not a theme I had thought much about until that time. But there can be no doubt that Christians suffer greatly when leaders mistreat a church and when churches mistreat leaders. I have concluded that there are four distinct areas in which spiritual abuse can arise. As we learn to recognise the characteristics of these destructive tendencies, we become better equipped to take practical, positive steps that will promote healthy patterns of leadership and church life.

1 **The problem of too much certainty.** Those Christians who have a high view of truth are most at risk of becoming over-dogmatic, baptising their own convictions with infallibility:

(a) *Extra-biblical dogmatism* is a characteristic danger for evangelicals. We may be tempted to assert that all our convictions are beyond dispute because they are 'all in the Bible'. While the Bible is unambiguous on the foundational doctrines of the faith, there are many issues on which those who take the Bible seriously come to different conclusions. This happens for example over women in leadership, believers' and infant baptism, just-war theory and outright pacifism, and pre-, post- and a-millennialist interpretations of the end times. Those evangelicals who crave too much certainty are tempted to assume that anyone who disagrees with them over any issue at all is biblically illiterate, stupid or wilfully disobedient.

(b) *Revelatory dogmatism* is a characteristic danger for charismatics, which arises because we take seriously the Holy Spirit's willingness to bring a prophetic word for today. The risk is that our every conviction, preference and vision become endowed with the authority of the Holy Spirit. To contradict the 'anointed servant of God' is to contradict the Holy Spirit and therefore to be spiritually disobedient or even in spiritual peril. Those charismatics who crave too much certainty are tempted to assume that anyone who disagrees with them is necessarily quenching the Holy Spirit.

(c) *Demonic dogmatism* is often connected with these first two extremes. The more we are convinced of the absolute authority of our own opinions, because the Bible or the Spirit has revealed everything to us, the more we are likely to suspect that any who oppose us must 'have a demon'. Someone who is a deliberate manipulator may use such language cynically and deceitfully, in order to strengthen their own authority among the gullible. But, sincere leaders who have come to take their own opinions far too seriously become just as dangerous. They can make a habit of 'discerning' demons in everyone who is hesitant or questioning of their leadership. Satan has little need to send legions of demons to mess up a church when over-dogmatic leaders are doing an excellent job on their own!

(d) *Denominational dogmatism* arises whenever we are tempted to believe that our churchmanship has cornered the market in truth or spiritual power. 'You worship God in your way,' is our generous appreciation of other Christians, 'while we worship God in his way.' If anyone describes their church as the only true Church, or their structure of church government as the only New Testament type, they reveal an ecclesiastical exclusivism that is dangerous and deluded. This dogmatism can arise in any church setting, ancient or modern. Some networks that describe themselves as non-denominational have a well-documented tendency to slip into this kind of sectarian exclusivity and elitism.

I suggest three practical steps to avoid excessive certainty. First, we need to get to know the Bible better, in all its rich expression of unity in diversity. Second, we need to seek a greater measure of personal humility. Third, we need to take to heart Paul's perspective, when he taught that we see through a glass darkly, and that the heart of the gospel is the *mystery* of God's redemptive love. The over-dogmatic actually understand very much less than they confidently suppose.

2 The problem of inappropriate leadership styles. Jesus deliberately excluded and warned against certain styles of leadership that came naturally in the Gentile world of his day. Sadly, similar excesses still arise in the Church today:

(a) *Authoritarian leaders* speak often about ruling the Church and the need for the people to submit. They love to lord it over people, which is precisely the style of leadership that Jesus repudiated (Mark 10:42–5). This style of leadership can find several distinct expressions. Some create a climate of dependency, in which the church members are entirely incapable of making any decisions, discerning God's will, or even engaging in worship and prayer, without the presence of their leader. The people are stripped of spiritual maturity.

Other authoritarian leaders de-skill those with whom they work. I remember meeting a highly gifted youth leader whose helpers never lasted more than a few months. His abilities were beyond doubt, but he was so over-bearing and critical that volunteers quickly concluded that they had nothing to contribute and so they soon dropped out.

Still others coerce their followers who are dominated and hectored into compliance. If the leader says give more, they do. If the leader says don't accept that promotion at work, they decline it. The people are stripped of their liberty and freedom to choose, like compliant citizens under a totalitarian regime.

(b) *Abdication of responsibility* is the opposite error. This happens when leaders fail to recognise that there are some things that they simply should not hand over or delegate. Such leaders present themselves as servants only. The result, almost inevitably, is that others rise up to fill the leadership vacuum. All too often the self-promoting leaders prove to be over-bearing people who swing the pendulum back towards the authoritarian extreme.

I suggest three practical steps to avoid unhelpful and even destructive styles of leadership. First, we need to get to know Jesus' leadership style better, by meditating upon the Gospels. We so easily lose sight of the paradox of servant leadership, in which leaders are certainly called to lead, but must learn to lead in the manner of a servant. Second, we need to follow the example of Paul, who was only comfortable with two kinds of boasting – the glory of Christ and his own weaknesses (2 Cor. 10:17, 11:30). Third, we need to recognise that in the New Testament there are no blueprints and no cloning – whether of churches, marriages, or personal Christian living. We need to understand leadership not in terms of having all the answers, but instead in terms of helping our fellow pilgrims on a journey into discipleship together.

3 The problem of destructive motivations. Just as certain leadership styles are excluded by the New Testament, our underlying motivation can become damaging to those we seek to lead. *The love of power* leads to the unsavoury aroma of church politics. *The love of prestige and status* results in Christian leaders indulging in pomp and ceremony, and so sinking into the mire of self-importance. *The need to be needed* can undermine any leader, who will continually seek appreciation to shore up their own self-worth. C. S. Lewis once wrote something like this, 'He was a man who lived for others. You could see the others he lived for by the hunted expression in their eyes.' Insecure leaders breed insecure churches, constantly looking over their shoulders for further proof of inadequacy.

I suggest three practical steps to uproot destructive motivations. First, we need to get to know ourselves better, with the help of the Holy Spirit, so that we can avoid becoming the unwitting victim of hidden inner needs. Second, we need to meditate upon the leadership of Moses and Peter. Both were naturally gifted leaders with grave character flaws who had to experience the pain of confronting their own leadership deficiencies before they could become effective servants of God. Third, we need to seek the priorities of the Sermon on the Mount, namely purity of heart and self-giving love, so that all our actions are shaped as much as possible by the motivations of true discipleship (and therefore of kingdom leadership) that were commended by Christ.

4 The problem of damaging experiences. Leaders can become imprisoned by the behaviour and attitudes of others, resulting in a characteristically cautious and wary posture – once bitten, twice shy. *Manipulators* constantly demand attention or try to impose their own priorities upon their leaders. They may make initial overtures of friendship, but eventually it becomes clear that the price tag of their friendship is that they demand to get their own

way in the church. *Power barons* instinctively employ in the church
the bullying, self-advancing or over-bearing methods they use at
work. *Lobbyists* always claim to speak on behalf of 'a lot of people
in the church, who are not at all happy with the way things are
going'. Sometimes 'a lot of people' means 'I was talking about this
with my wife at breakfast – and the dog and the budgie were both
in the room at the time'. *Specialists in negativity* always have
something to complain about. Some make a habit of sending letters
of complaint on a regular basis, while others take to sitting in the
back row on Sunday mornings, scowling through every sermon.
These attitudes often wear leaders down. The first flushes of
enthusiasm and optimism erode quickly. In their place, the bruised
leader can become increasingly weary, cynical and defensive, afraid
to trust people any more.

I suggest three practical steps to avoid becoming imprisoned by
destructive experiences. First, we need to keep short accounts when
it comes to forgiveness. Every time we pray the Lord's prayer we
are called to the discipline of forgiveness as a continuing practice
of healthy discipleship. Second, we need to develop a circle of real
friends, who can always be relied upon to provide encouragement,
support and appropriate criticism, with no strings attached. Third,
we need to find a circle of fellow leaders with whom we can share
honestly. It helps enormously to receive the counsel and prayers of
others who have faced similar pressures.

Spiritual abuse is real and desperately damaging. But with these
practical steps we can minimise the disasters and maximise our
potential for good. The Christian Church needs to liberate leaders
into the tasks of servant leadership. At the same time we need
Christian leaders of all kinds to understand that their task is not to
dominate, but rather to liberate the people of God, in order that
everyone really can fulfil their potential in Christ. Leaders with
the ability to liberate others into spiritual maturity need to develop
these four distinctive qualities: *A sense of calling* – we need to ensure
that we do not lose sight of the One who called and the ministry to
which he has called us. *A sense of purpose* – we need to know what
we are seeking to accomplish, under God, and when and how we
are going to attempt to do it. *A sense of proportion* – we need to

recognise that when problems arise they are rarely the end of the world, even if they seem that way at first. *A sense of humour* – those who have learned to laugh at life stay fresh. Those who have learned to laugh at themselves are protected from that most terrible danger of Christian leadership – taking ourselves far too seriously.

Paul faced spiritual abuse at Corinth, when the so-called super-apostles came to town and attempted to undermine and discredit his ministry. He identified four strands to their abusive leadership (2 Cor. 11:20): *They were dominating* – Paul warns that they are sure to 'enslave' and 'exploit' their followers. *They were manipulative* – twisters of truth, their consistent pattern is to 'take advantage' of circumstances and people. *They were self-serving* – far from servant leadership, they were inclined to 'push themselves forward'. *They were aggressive* – Paul reminds the Corinthians of a 'slap in the face', which may have been a literal, physical blow, or possibly an all-out verbal assault.

So why were the Corinthians taken in, at least for a time, and why have Christians been taken in by abusive leadership ever since? Because such leadership is domineering and manipulative, it can be hard to resist. One person I spoke to explained to me that she was made to feel as if she was opposing God and undermining the vision of her church by not going along 100 per cent with every decision the leaders announced. Some people seem to be particularly susceptible to abusive leadership. It gives them a sense of confidence, security and direction. All the uncertainty is taken out of life and someone else makes all the hard decisions for you. In the short term, some find this very reassuring as they adopt a child–parent relationship with their church leaders. Eventually, however, they are sure to realise that this is a false security. If they don't escape, ultimately it will become soul-destroying.

Paul's own leadership style seeks to reflect the pattern of Christ. Where there was disagreement, he sought to demolish arguments, not people (2 Cor. 10:4–5). His overriding concern was to build up, not pull down (2 Cor. 10:8). Faced with the self-assertive boasting of the misguided 'super-apostles', Paul was concerned not to commend himself, but rather to be commended by the Lord (2 Cor. 10:18). Because Paul worked hard to rescue the church at Corinth from spiritual abuse, his leadership style provides the biblical antidote to a style of leadership that, in Jesus' words, 'lords it over' the people of God.

Foot-washing leadership

When Jesus washed his disciples' feet, it was a glorious example of servant leadership in action (John 13:4–5). The love that would take Jesus to the cross is symbolised in this simple act of practical care. In the hot and dusty world of the ancient Middle East, in the days when travel by foot was commonplace, it was normal practice to ensure that your guests had an opportunity to wash their feet before settling down to food. On this particular day, the evening meal was about to be served when everyone's feet were still hot and dusty. So Jesus did the honours.

To become a servant leader does not mean that we have to abandon leadership altogether. Jesus identified a problem and seized the initiative with an effective solution. He not only dealt with the immediate need, but turned it into an acted parable, a memorable moment that would stay with his followers as a telling demonstration of a radically different kind of leadership. His followers knew that he provided unparalleled spiritual leadership, but now he demonstrated that this did not mean he was too other-worldly to get his hands dirty. Every moment of this episode is not a repudiation of leadership but rather an affirmation of leadership, restyled in the way of Jesus' own servanthood. Jesus invited his disciples to begin to discover what it means to become leaders with servant hearts.

This is a paradox and a mystery with which the Church has struggled ever since. At one extreme, some churches are tempted to repudiate leadership altogether, treating 'leader' almost as a dirty word. At the other extreme, some champion strong leadership so much that they create a kind of hyper-clericalism, in which the leaders contribute almost everything and the chief task of the congregation is to be passive and grateful. Both extremes are grievously inadequate attempts to express Jesus' values. His leadership is unmistakable. His servanthood is astonishing. And he calls us, whatever the extent of our responsibilities at home, church and work, to take the creative risk of seeking to combine the two:

Now that I, your Lord and Teacher, have washed your feet, you also should wash one another's feet. I have set you an example that you should do as I have done for you. I tell you the truth, no servant is greater than his master, nor is a messenger greater than the one who sent him. Now that you know these things, you will be blessed if you do them. (John 13:14–17)

Servants of the Church

Paul described himself as a servant of the gospel (Col. 1:23) and a servant of the Church (Col. 1:25). As an apostolic leader and as a Christian believer, Paul is determined that servanthood is centre stage. He is a servant of the Church in five distinct ways: *In his witness*, wherever he has travelled he has sought to make Christ known (Col. 1:25–7). *In his suffering*, he has not swerved from faithful service (Col. 1:24). *In his teaching*, he has sought to proclaim the 'word of God in its fulness' (Col. 1:25–7), which requires a disciplined dedication to proclaim the full counsel of the Scriptures, the whole truth and nothing but the truth. *In his leadership*, he has sought to present 'everyone perfect in Christ' (Col. 1:28). *In his consistent hard work*, he has been energised for service, equipped to keep on serving by the Spirit of Christ, who powerfully sustains him in his servanthood (Col. 1:29).

To present everyone 'perfect' – that is, mature in Christ (Col. 1:28) – speaks of a leadership style that is empowering. Paul is not willing to instil passivity, subservience or over-dependence. When a gardener plants a young tree, it needs to be staked. Otherwise it has no protection from fierce winds and could be destroyed. If the stake is too tall, the tree will grow weak. It must be able to move in the wind in order to grow strong and stand on its own. No stake and it will snap. Too much stake and it will never become a mature tree.

Even so, wise Christian leadership provides just enough support for people to grow into stability and maturity. The preacher wants to open up the Scriptures in such a way that genuinely biblical insights continue to enrich believers' lives when the preacher has long since been forgotten. The counsellor wants to assist people to come to a place where they no longer need the counsellor's help. The parent wants to provide just enough support to help his or her children advance into adult independence, supported but not over-protected.

Servant leaders who want to present everyone mature in Christ will develop a distinctive leadership style. The central emphasis cannot be, 'Look how much I can do for you', but rather, 'See how much you can do in Christ'. The key to the remarkable expansion of the Pauline churches in the first generation was that Paul believed in the believers. Despite the many mistakes of doctrine and practice that his letters often needed to tackle, Paul persistently helped Christians develop a 'can do' attitude because he was confident that the Holy Spirit really had been given to every believer. Since the leaders had no monopoly of the Spirit, they could claim no monopoly of ministry, nor could they have any excuse for cultivating 'lean-to' Christians, incapable of standing on their own feet in Christ.

Our fulfilment as leaders, whether of a church or a denomination, an organisation or a home group, or indeed within the family, is meant to be found not simply in the fulfilment of our own potential, but more deeply in the fulfilment of those we are seeking to lead into the fullness of Christian maturity. The ambition of servant leaders is not to produce our own mini-disciples, dependent upon us and clones of ourselves, but instead to release others into a whole-life discipleship that is stable, strong and mature.

Chapter 12

Complete in Christ

Colossians 2:1–3:10
WHEN YOU SEE the massed competitors at the end of a marathon, their faces are etched with agony and ecstasy. The agony of pushing themselves to the limit, and the ecstasy of crossing the finish line. Claire's ambition is to run the marathon one day. Mine is to run it never! Paul described his own ministry as a 'struggle' on behalf of the churches he served (Col. 2:1–10). Literally the word means that he 'agonised' for them, just as he wrote that Epaphras was 'agonising' for the Church in prayer (Col. 4:12). Communists used to speak of 'the struggle', a determined effort to live as people of destiny. Even so, Paul knew that serving Christ was the overriding 'struggle' of his life. He worked hard in the defence and advance of the gospel. He worked hard in prayer. He worked hard in his prison experience, enduring suffering and the threat of martyrdom. He worked hard in his composition of this letter. And he worked hard to bring others to maturity in Christ. Paul's agony was his hard work and persecution, his ecstasy was to live a life worthy of the Lord and to see other Christians fulfil their potential in Christ.

Established in the faith
Three-legged milking stools are a simple design that has stood the test of time. Just as the triangle is a shape of great strength in any engineering project, the three legs of a milking stool make a safe seat. Paul reveals that his hard work on behalf of the Colossians has a threefold purpose: he longs for them to be encouraged in heart, united in love, and have a complete understanding of the gospel (Col. 2:2–5). Like the three legs of the milking stool, we

need all three qualities if we are to enjoy stability and growth as disciples.

Encouraged in heart speaks of the experiential dimension of living faith. The word translated as 'encouraged' is *parakaleo*, which means comfort and strengthen. It's connected with the word used of the Holy Spirit in John's Gospel, when he is described as another Counsellor or Comforter of the same kind as Jesus (John 14–16). This encouragement comes from God and has a double impact. He comes to us in tender mercy to bind our wounds. And he comes to fire us up, to quicken our zeal so that our eagerness is renewed to live boldly and decisively, making a significant impact for Christ.

The Greek word for 'heart' is *kardia*, familiar to many of us because of the phrase 'cardiac arrest'. For us, phrases such as 'heart experience' and 'heart knowledge' speak mainly of our emotional and intuitive life. For the Jews, the heart had a much wider significance, meaning our inner life in its entirety, our will and emotions, thoughts and affections. They considered the heart to be the centre of our personality. To be 'encouraged in heart' therefore includes our emotions, but speaks of an encouragement that has an impact that is wider than our emotions. To be encouraged in heart is to be inwardly strengthened. The gospel has the power to inwardly fortify believers who have become fainthearted or discouraged.

United in love speaks of the relational dimension of faith. United can mean knit together or bound together. When I first entered publishing, the production director was at pains to demonstrate to me the difference between an American and a British hardback book. Taking hold of one page in an American edition, he shook it and it was immediately torn from the book which fell to the floor. Grasping one page in a British edition, he shook it just as vigorously and the entire book continued to hang by the single leaf. (Please don't try this at home: as modern production processes become standardised worldwide, it is less and less likely that new hardbacks from British publishers will be able to take the strain. You have been warned!) Many Christians use their Bibles as a loose-leaf filing system. If they drop them, several months of notice sheets, Bible reading notes and conference memorabilia are scattered across the floor. It's only the actual pages of the Bible that have been truly bound together. Even so, when we come to faith in

Christ, we are no longer loosely associating with the Church, we are truly grafted into the living vine.

My dramatic introduction to the durability of traditional British hardbacks was very memorable. But a better illustration of being bound together in love is the old-fashioned rag rug. Peasant families would not want to waste any scraps of material. When clothing was too tattered for continued use, it would be torn into strips and woven into a multi-coloured rug. The pieces were bound together, so that the rug could endure hard wear. But every piece retained its original colour and pattern. This expresses well the Church at its best: unity without uniformity, belonging not conformity. That's why coffee after a service, church lunches and social events are an integral part of Christian discipleship.

Church is not meant to be an event that we attend as isolated individuals, where we sit alone in our own pew, and from which we depart as soon as possible at the end of the service. Church is meant to be experienced as a network of loving relationships in which we all thrive in a climate of encouragement and mutual support. In a society where lives are ever more fragmented, with a declining sense of community, little opportunity to get to know neighbours, and increasingly fragile relationships in the home, few things could be more attractive about a church than a real sense of belonging. Ann told me about a recent conversation at work. Her colleagues were amazed that she spent time with people of different generations: for most of them, life outside work was spent in a single-generation world, with no opportunity to mix beyond their own age group. This is a glorious example of the power of the gospel to restore our potential. Made in the image of the triune God – three persons in the eternal community of divine love – we are given in Christ new opportunities to discover and enjoy being united in love.

The full riches of complete understanding speaks of the doctrinal dimension of discipleship (Col. 2:2). 'Complete' doesn't suggest that our knowledge must be exhaustive, but we will be helped enormously if our grasp of basic doctrine is well-balanced and rounded. The false teachers of Colosse were wanting to suggest that there was some kind of further revelation, beyond Christ. Paul flatly contradicts them by reminding the Christians that in Christ are found 'all the treasures of wisdom and knowledge'. The false teachers wanted to establish a premier league of 'higher disciples', initiates in a higher knowledge. Paul's insistence that full riches and all treasure are found in Christ is emphatic. There is no need to add anything extra, for Christ is all we need.

Here, then, is the three-legged stool of Christian maturity: the experiential, relational and doctrinal dimensions. Churches have often been tempted to emphasise one element at the expense of another. Doctrine without experience leads to dry-as-dust theories, information without power. Doctrine without unity leads to divisiveness, a sectarian suspicion that all other groups of Christians are almost certainly, and almost always, unsound. Experience without doctrine leads to a subjective chaos in which anything goes so long as there's a good experience attached. Relationships without doctrine lead to saying it doesn't matter what anyone believes, so long as we are being relational with them. Experience without relationships leads to everyone doing their own thing, having their own private walk with God without ever committing to belonging to the Church of Christ. No wonder Paul prayed that we would know the fullness of Christian discipleship in all three dimensions. On their own, each of these three is inadequate. Together they bring us the interactive power of the presence, the love and the truth of God.

The bedrock of Christ

Having affirmed the importance of all three dimensions of discipleship, Paul emphasises the sure foundation of Christ. Inner encouragement and unity in love are both vital, but it is a clear grasp of Christ himself that makes these two possible. Brazilian football commentators at the World Cup are almost always 'over the top'. Their enthusiasm and devotion is intense, so that when Brazil score, their excitement reaches fever pitch as they scream a single word – 'G-O-A-L!!' Paul's equivalent verbal trick is not to shout, but to pile up phrase upon phrase to express the immensity of God and his revelation in Christ. He speaks of the 'full riches of complete understanding' and then, almost immediately, of 'all the treasures of wisdom and knowledge' (Col. 2:2, 3). The overlap and repetition is a way of indicating that words cannot fully express the super-abundance of all we have in Christ. He is truly the incomparable One, and knowledge of Christ is the bedrock upon which we can build a life worth living.

Paul explains that this fullness of treasure is 'hidden' in Christ (Col. 2:3). The word has a double significance. First it recognises that the revelation of Christ is veiled. When he walked the earth, his identity was not apparent to everyone. And beyond the incarnation, in which God's presence is both revealed and yet veiled, there is the intrinsic mystery of God who reveals himself to us, and yet must inevitably remain beyond our full comprehension. That's one reason why false teaching can seem attractive: it offers to tie up all the loose ends where biblical Christianity acknowledges mystery, uncertainty and the limits of our understanding.

The second meaning of 'hidden' is that wisdom and knowledge are deposited or stored up in Christ. Don't trouble to look elsewhere. Don't be seduced by cults of personality or claims of higher revelations. The only place to find God's wisdom and knowledge is in the person and gospel of Jesus Christ. The Jews had traditionally claimed that all the treasures of wisdom and knowledge could be found in the law. Paul takes up that theme and strengthens it: all that wisdom and more is ours and can be found in Christ Jesus.

Some years ago I was due to catch an early morning plane back home from the United States. When I went to check out from my hotel and retrieve my passport, an unexpected problem arose. The manager had phoned in sick and no one on duty could remember where the spare key to the safe was kept. I had the air ticket, and was within a couple of metres of my passport, but for the next twenty minutes what was mine was inaccessible. There are no such inefficiencies in the divine economy. God's wisdom and knowledge are hidden in Christ and they are made fully available to his followers, as we reflect upon his life and teaching and as we receive his loving presence by the Holy Spirit. Here is the heart of Paul's apostolic message and the key ingredient of Christian maturity: Christ is all we need!

Rooted and built up

When I was learning to drive, my instructor had a favourite phrase: 'You need to practise this for the test, but everyone ignores it afterwards.' Paul's understanding of the connection between theory and practice couldn't be more different. In conversion all we need is Christ, and exactly the same is true in our continuing discipleship. Paul urges the Colossians not to be swayed or distracted so that they would end up majoring on minors: 'Just as you received Christ Jesus as Lord, continue to live in him . . .' (Col. 2:6).

Receiving, keeping and passing on is a very important part of Paul's understanding of the Christian life. He passed on Jesus' words at the Last Supper, just as he had received them (1 Cor. 11:23). He urges Timothy to keep the pattern of sound teaching he had received from Paul (2 Tim. 1:13), and in turn to entrust this 'good deposit' to the next generation of leaders and teachers (2 Tim. 2:2). Here we see the New Testament notion of apostolic succession, not as a line of bishops, but rather as an unbroken tradition of teachers and churches who declare, preserve and pass on the apostolic good news. Irrespective of denomination or stream, every church where Jesus is proclaimed as Lord belongs within the apostolic Church of Jesus Christ.

I recently came across one church stream that stated they were planting a church in a particular town because there was 'no New Testament-type church there'. In fact, there were several churches in that town proclaiming Jesus as Lord and holding to biblical orthodoxy. I didn't object to the church plant: in most parts of Britain there is a need for many more churches if we are to reach the nation effectively. What did concern me was the attempt to monopolise the phrase 'New Testament-type church' for churches of their particular style of organisation. This is sectarian arrogance and needs to be avoided at all costs. Instead of claiming that our kind of church is the only proper one, which is the most distasteful form of hyper-denominationalism, we need to accept warmly our partnership in the gospel with all who declare Jesus as Lord.

Paul encourages us to continue to live *in Christ*, rather than to live *for him* dutifully but in an impersonal way. Our privilege is not just to serve Christ at a distance, but to walk with him even as we serve him. To live *in him* recognises that Christ becomes our environment for wholeness in life and spiritual vitality. Like a deep sea diver who is dependent on their oxygen supply in an alien environment, we need to learn to depend on the Spirit of God in the midst of our daily living. Some garden plants have to be grafted on to a different rootstock to keep them healthy and vigorous and to ensure that they grow to an ideal size. At the time of the grafting, two separate plants are pushed together. Once the graft has taken, they become one. The energy of the rootstock is transferred directly into the flowering and fruiting stems. To live in Christ means to continue to acknowledge our dependence upon him. He's the air that we breathe, the energy that keeps us growing, the rootstock that brings fruitfulness to our lives.

This invitation to a continued intimacy with Christ, to life as a journey in the company of God, is reinforced by a series of metaphors that express how dependence on Christ is the key to continued spiritual growth. The first metaphor is agricultural – 'rooted in him' (Col. 2:7). Novice gardeners will often buy a plant from a garden centre, place it in their garden at home, and then watch it die slowly over the next few weeks. If a plant has been growing vigorously, it can easily be pot bound. When it's knocked out of its pot, the roots are thoroughly congested and twisted round and round in the shape of the pot. Once roots have established this growth pattern, the risk is that they will keep on growing round in circles even after the plant has been planted in your garden. The roots need gently teasing out, so that they are ready to make life-giving contact with the garden soil. Healthy roots will go deep, searching out nutrients for healthy growth. Even so, to be rooted in Christ means that our roots go deep into him, so that we are anchored in the face of a storm, well nourished spiritually, and strengthened to live life to the full. We therefore need to ask ourselves a practical question from time to time: How well rooted are we in Christ?

Paul's second metaphor is architectural – 'built up in him' (Col. 2:7). An architect must have long-term vision, seeing the end before the beginning so that foundations are built sufficiently deep and strong to support the entire edifice. When architects look at an existing building, they have been trained to see possibilities of renovation and development that are completely invisible to the untrained eye. To be built up in Christ speaks of our lives as a construction site, where Christ is the Master Architect, capable of bringing out a potential we have never even seen in ourselves. He develops us, improves us, and moves us towards becoming a completed building. Just as the Golden Gate Bridge always has painters and engineers at work upon it, our lives are a perpetual building site, as God continues to renovate and develop us.

Paul's third metaphor is legal – 'strengthened in the faith' (Col. 2:7). The word translated as 'strengthened' means sealed, made binding, established, settled for action. God is looking for believers who won't be content with being saved, but who long to maximise their impact for good upon his world. When God seals our lives with the gift of salvation he urges us to settle for nothing less than whole-life discipleship – now go for it!

Here, then, is a double task for every local church. First we have a responsibility to hand on the unchanging gospel to new believers and the rising generations. They will need to find their own ways of expressing worship and developing the life of the Church, but the gospel itself needs to be passed on complete and untarnished. Second, we need to create an environment that promotes personal spiritual growth. This doesn't mean standardisation, narrowness or shallow conformity in our understanding of discipleship. We are individual plants rooted in Christ, not clones. We are individual buildings built up in Christ, not franchise outlets that all look the same. The climate of personal growth that we need to develop must give space for individual discovery and expression, for we each have a personal journey of growth to make in Christ. We are not meant to get stuck after the first few months or years of Christian faith, slip into neutral and park at the roadside, marking time with a discipleship that is going nowhere.

Paul urges us to stay focused on Christ, keeping him centre stage in our priorities and values. He also encourages us to retain the expectation that the Christian life is a journey of discovery in which we can experience continued personal growth. If you feel more like a dried flower than a plant in full bloom, more like a tumbledown ruin than a building that is enjoying continuous development and improvement, it's time to ask Christ to renovate your discipleship and restore you to healthy growth.

Fullness in Christ

There are three common ways in which Christians can become susceptible to misleading promises of a higher spiritual life. When we are keen, our eagerness can make us gullible. When we feel insecure, we are easily impressed by someone else's apparent superior spiritual vitality. When we are captive to this world's ways of thinking, we accept assumptions that have very little to do with the Bible. We can't say for sure how much the Colossians suffered from gullibility and being too easily impressed. We do know that they were attempting to build their discipleship on non-biblical foundations, which is why Paul warned them against ways of thinking that were 'hollow', 'deceptive', and based on 'human tradition' rather than biblical revelation (Col. 2:8). He urged them to be on their guard, and we need to be just as careful not to dilute or contaminate the gospel with alien teaching.

Spiritual maturity always begins at the same place – a resounding affirmation of the uniqueness and supremacy of Christ. Paul calls the Colossians back to the magnetic north of true discipleship by reminding them of the definitive miracle of the incarnation: 'in Christ all the fulness of the Deity lives in bodily form' (Col. 2:9). The incarnation and resurrection are historical realities. They really happened and many eyewitnesses were still alive when Paul wrote his letters. The incarnation is a saving necessity. Fully God and fully man, Christ bridges the gap and makes reconciliation available. The incarnation is the only reasonable explanation of Jesus. His teaching, character, healings, deliverance and resurrection all point to his divinity. That he ate food, needed sleep, showed emotions (including weeping at a friend's tomb), bled and died all point to his real humanity. The incarnation is a mystery, in which we affirm the truth and embrace the paradox, without being able to explain precisely how God accomplished this unique miracle. God didn't send his Son for a long Easter weekend to become the atoning sacrifice and return hotfoot to heaven. For more than thirty years, the Son of God walked this earth with skin and bone, affirming in this most intimate of ways the value and potential of human life.

Paul emphasises the centrality of the incarnation because it cuts across the many prejudices and errors of the super-spirituality that was starting to infect the Colossian church. He then adds a corollary which is just as miraculous and extraordinary: 'and you have been given fulness in Christ' (Col. 2:10). Clearly we are not provided with fullness of deity, but rather with fullness of salvation, grace and life. Paul's use of the passive mood – 'you have been given' – emphasises that this is not something we can win for ourselves, but is an extravagant provision of God. The tense is perfect, which means that fullness in Christ has been made available to us through a single, decisive event in the past that has a continuing impact in the present. In short, Paul is not calling the Colossians to aim at, seek or strive after fullness, but instead is declaring that this is the freely provided inheritance and entitlement of every Christian believer. All that was Christ's by birthright becomes ours by the power of his cross. Here is true and lasting Christian confidence, not the arrogance that would presume to say, 'I don't need anyone else.' But instead, the security in grace that allows us to declare, 'All that I need, even though I don't deserve it, is found and made freely available in Christ.'

People suffer from a vast array of feelings of inferiority: too young or too old, no good at sport, no good at exams, too tall or too short, too fat or too thin, too talkative or too quiet. We judge and feel judged because of our social background, our income, whether we are in paid employment, our gender, our ethnic grouping and our marital status. This glorious promise of the New Testament cuts across all kinds of social hierarchy. Christian disciples should never want to look down on others; we need to learn to build everyone up, affirming that they too have been given fullness in Christ.

As for ourselves, fullness in Christ can be like a gift token we have never used or an inheritance we have never claimed. The full abundance of everlasting life has been provided for every believer in Christ, but so often we make do with half measures. Much of the New Testament can be summed up in the invitation to 'become what you are'. Instead of living our Christian lives in second gear, we can gather the confidence to receive and to put into practice the fullness of all that Christ has already made available for his disciples. These two glorious truths are a matching pair: all fullness is found in Christ and, as a direct result, we have been given fullness in Christ. Now this is a provision of God that is surely worth getting excited about! There really is no need to look elsewhere or feel insecure in your faith. All that we need is found in Christ.

Singleness and wholeness

We cannot leave the theme of fullness in Christ without affirming that this applies fully to both singles and marrieds. In the medieval period, the Church elevated celibate singleness as the higher calling and the only way to be a truly spiritual Christian. The modern Protestant Church has often reversed that prejudice, and has often tended to marginalise single people. Many churches state categorically that they would not want a single minister. Others have never had a single person on their leadership team. Some expressly state that home groups will always be led by married couples. Since Jesus himself was single, such attitudes would be laughable if they did not cause so much distress.

The great irony of our society is that a high percentage of singles wish they were married and a high percentage of marrieds, judging by the divorce rates, wish they were single. In 1999, government policy on building new homes has accepted the projection that an increasing number of adults will be living alone over the next twenty years. There are, of course, many kinds of singleness. Some are single and have never married. Some are single, have never married, but have lived with one or more partners in the past. Some are single and divorced. Some are single through bereavement. Some are not single in the rest of their life, but are 'church singles', since their partner is not a believer and never attends church. The experiences of single people are therefore complex and diverse, and we must be careful of the dangers of over-generalisation.

There is also a need for great sensitivity, since some singles carry a private burden of deeply painful experiences. (It is vital that churches are just as careful when speaking about single parents, since at least four kinds of life experience result in these circumstances: never married, divorced, separated, bereaved.) One helpful and salutary step for many churches is to analyse their own directory. When I have invited churches to do this, around half the adults attending were found to be single. Until the leaders made this discovery, they had blithely assumed that the overwhelming majority of the congregation were married.

Pressures on singles

Single people report several pressures that they often endure. The first, usually at weddings and engagement parties, is voiced as a question: 'Do you think you'll be next?' It's meant to be humorous and well-intended, but with repetition it soon wears thin. Just as relatives and friends voice this question, it's also often heard at church. What's more, if all the illustrations at church come from married life, whether verbal in the preaching or pictorial in clip art, a consistent, even if unintentional, message is conveyed that marriage is better, normal, and more or less automatic. As a result, single people can be made to feel second best.

The second pressure can come from friends and also from the media – 'You're not still a virgin, are you?' Virginity is treated as an embarrassing disease which needs to be cured as quickly as possible, rather than a virtue to be treasured. There is a pressure upon people somehow to prove themselves through sexual activity. Hollywood frequently propagates two myths: that sex is instantly and always fulfilling; and that sex has no emotional price tag. Christians need to emphasise that the Bible is not anti-sex, but does restrict love-making to the place where it is enriching, not damaging – that is, the marriage relationship. Many kinds of insinuation are made against the person who is a virgin, from frigidity to latent homo-sexuality. Many a manipulative boyfriend has tried to trick a girl into having sex with the line, 'If you loved me, you would do what I want.' The best reply to such pressure is something like this: 'If you loved me, you wouldn't keep asking.' We need to get the pride back into virginity.

The third pressure comes from marrieds who blithely declare, 'You must have so much free time.' Obviously a disposable income goes further without children to provide for, but many regular chores take just as long for one person as for a couple. Some who are single love to baby-sit, but not all do. It is a great shame if the only significant social contact between singles and marrieds is to hand over temporary care of young children.

The Bible and singleness

Jesus emphasised that there are several quite different experiences of singleness (Matt. 19:12). Some are single by nature, never wanting anything else. Some are single by calling, making an active choice for the sake of the gospel. I have known some missionaries make that decision, knowing that long-term service in an isolated area probably means they will not meet a life partner. Others have turned down a non-Christian partner rather than enter a marriage where conflicting priorities are built in from day one. Some are single through circumstances, neither by preference nor by active choice; it's just that it's worked out that way so far. For this kind of single person, there is an uncertainty in simply not knowing whether singleness is for a season or for life. The television character Ally McBeal is by no means alone in her acute awareness that the biological clock is ticking remorselessly.

Paul took a very positive view of singleness (1 Cor. 7:27–8; 32–5). He encouraged singles not to go looking for a partner (1 Cor. 7:27). This pinpoints the danger of a constant, underlying longing or anxiety, where finding a partner becomes our dominant concern. I have met people trying to live that way, and it seems to me to be nothing less than soul destroying. Paul also stressed that the married life is often far from easy. Marriage brings many troubles (1 Cor. 7:28) and leads to divided interests, since the married will inevitably be concerned for their partner as well as their Lord (1 Cor. 7:33–5). Paul stressed that he certainly did not consider it wrong to marry, but he was persuaded that, for some people, singleness can actually bring the greater happiness (1 Cor. 7:40). This teaching is a healthy corrective to the over-promotion of marriage in some parts of the Church today. We must be careful not to confuse our own preference with what is God's best for every believer.

Jesus is our model of human fulfilment. He is not only the definitive revelation of the character and saving purposes of God. He is also the most complete person, the most whole and the most fully alive, who has ever walked the earth. Since he was not married and died a virgin he provides a direct repudiation of the great myths in our society: you don't have to get married, live with someone, or be sexually active in order to be a fulfilled and complete person. Our Model and Master lived and died single, which is a rebuke to our prejudices and can be an enormous comfort and inspiration to single people. We should also emphasise that Jesus enjoyed close friendships with both men and women. His chosen lifestyle was far from isolated.

Fullness in Christ is provided for every believer, irrespective of our marital status. We are all made complete in Christ, who can liberate us from destructive pressures and rescue us from every kind of negative self-image. We cannot stress it too strongly: single people and married people receive fullness in Christ in exactly the same measure. Irrespective of our marital status, all that we need is found in Christ.

Chapter 13

Generous Giving

2 Corinthians 8–9

THE MOST DEVELOPED New Testament teaching on giving is found in 2 Corinthians 8–9, which provides us with seven key principles: we are called to giving that is voluntary, generous, responsible, planned, proportionate, it will have mutual benefits, and it needs to come from the heart.

Our giving should be voluntary

Paul was facing an awkward problem. The Corinthians had been quick off the mark in offering to take part in his collection among the Gentile churches to assist the church in Judea in a time of hardship. It was a great act of kindness from Gentile to Jewish Christians showing their oneness in Christ, expressing generosity in a time of practical need, and demonstrating that the new generation of churches had no intention of disregarding the Jewish congregations, many of which had been established before the Gentiles began turning to Christ. Unfortunately, the Corinthians had been swift with enthusiastic words and slow to take action. These chapters are Paul's attempt to spur them on to generous giving, and he combines three elements: the inspiring example of the Macedonians, biblical incentives to generosity (supremely the cross of Christ), and practical suggestions.

When Paul cites the Macedonian generosity, he stresses that they took the initiative to be sacrificial in their giving – 'entirely on their own' (2 Cor. 8:3). Similarly, he avoids putting undue pressure upon the Corinthians, explaining that he is 'not commanding you' (2 Cor. 8:8). He insists that within the local church each individual must be free to make their own decisions – 'not under compulsion'

– handing over what they have 'decided in his heart to give' (2 Cor. 9:7). Here we see an absolute repudiation of any attempt to treat personal giving like a church taxation system. The right of the individual to make their own decisions, free from any kind of interference or duress, is affirmed.

This rules out two kinds of extremism: local church treasurers and finance teams can offer to help people complete forms, but have no right to tell people what they ought to give. Paul does not allow us to make any particular level of giving obligatory. Second, there is no excuse for the extended appeal for money that has blighted some Christian gatherings, where the introduction to the offering becomes as long as the main talk, and where the congregation are prevailed upon, whether through excitement or a sense of guilt, to give under considerable emotional duress. It's understandable why Christian leaders may be tempted to try too hard to extract money from their audience. Perhaps their own income or the advance of their vision and ministry is dependent upon a budget being met through the offering. Or perhaps they are frustrated by the instinctive stinginess of some Christians, happy to spend much money on themselves but reluctant to release more than loose change for the alleviation of need and the advance of God's kingdom.

Paul's example is an invitation to Christian leaders to exercise faith rather than impose pressure. We need to learn to take the risk of encouraging people to make an offering that is generous because it is free-will rather than obligatory. Money should not be extracted from Christians like a pearl from an oyster – forcibly and painfully. Our offering should be a pressure-free zone, because people must always come first.

Our giving should be generous

The Macedonians amazed Paul because their positive and generous attitudes contradicted what could be expected of people in their circumstances (2 Cor. 8:2–3). They were suffering a trial that was 'severe' and yet their joy was 'overflowing'. They faced poverty that was 'extreme' and yet their generosity was 'rich'. Far from making an excuse out of their own pressing needs and lack of funds, they gave 'as much as they were able and even beyond their ability'.

So captivated were they by gospel values that giving away their money had become an eager privilege rather than a reluctant obligation.

Paul is not attempting to compel or shame the Corinthians into giving, but rather to inspire them. He therefore presents the example of Christ as the ultimate spur to generosity. Though he was rich with the riches of heaven, he humbled himself and became poor, so that we might enter into eternal riches through his poverty (2 Cor. 8:9). We who are rich in eternal life can afford to be liberal with material wealth, which is no longer our ultimate concern. Christ's wonderful example of self-sacrifice for the sake of the lost can inspire us to new heights of generosity in material things. His self-giving love has saved us, and now our self-giving love in his service can begin to transform our world.

Our giving should be responsible

Although the need in Judaea was great and immediate, Paul and his team chose to leave out the Macedonians from the general appeal to the Gentile churches. They considered them too poor to be able to help and wanted to protect them in their poverty from unhelpful pressure or from any sense of an obligation that they would be unable to meet. This is a far cry from the pressure tactics of some over-zealous Christians who seem intent on extracting the last cent from their poorest supporters. Once the Macedonians made a genuine request to be able to contribute, wise pastoral consideration then respected their freedom to give. Forced giving would have been inappropriate. Voluntary giving, even from the very poor, was welcomed and appreciated.

Paul's team also had the wisdom to build in safeguards for the management of the gift. This was just as well, since someone at Corinth seems to have started a rumour that the offering was not being handled properly. Paul was able to explain that the offering had an independent 'minder', appointed by the churches, who travelled with the missionary team and looked after the money that was being raised (2 Cor. 8:18–19). Sometimes Christians object to 'doing things by the book' on the grounds that we should be able to trust one another, but Paul knew the wisdom not only of doing what is right, but of being seen to do it. He therefore kept a distance between his team's upfront ministry and the management of the money. Both these principles are very sound. We need to ensure that our church accounts are properly managed and scrutinised. We also need to ensure that the confidential information that has to be known by a finance team is kept well away from the wider leadership team of a local church. My own view has always been that it is much better for church leaders not to know any details about the larger financial donors, because such information may colour our judgement about the developing vision and priorities of that particular church.

Our giving should be planned

The Corinthians were suffering from an all too common problem. When they first heard about the offering Paul was organising, they were first in line with an initial gift and with promises to give a lot more. As the months went by they found it hard to part with their money, either because they were impulsive or because they were disorganised. Paul had realised their difficulty, so he had encouraged them in a previous letter to set aside a sum of money on the first day of every week, saving it up for the planned offering (1 Cor. 16:2).

As we head towards a cashless society, our giving also needs to be planned. Many companies now prefer consumers to pay bills by direct debit and standing order, so that the money is taken direct from our bank accounts. Some churches have developed a small change mentality. The offering bag comes round and we check our pockets to see whether we have something to give. Most of our shopping is now done with plastic rather than cash. The pound in our pocket is worth so much less than in previous generations that a handful of coins simply does not go very far. For those who use standing orders to pay their regular bills, it makes good sense to organise our regular giving to church in a similar way. We urgently need to take away the emphasis from offering bags because they encourage a small change, disorganised approach to regular giving by Christians.

For some churches no kind of meeting is complete without an offering. It's like an airport tax: every time you enter the building there's more to pay. Far from encouraging responsible, generous giving by Christians, this reinforces the small change mentality: never enter the building without some coins in your pocket or purse, because an offering bag is sure to come your way! As for non-Christians, this kind of experience reinforces the suspicion that the church is always after your money. We need more planned giving and less scooping up of small change.

The great hurdle to planned giving for some people is not the concept, nor deciding how much to give. They are simply allergic to filling in forms. Give them a form to take home and it is sure to enter a black hole from where forms have never been known to re-emerge. The best solution to form-phobia that I have come across is for a church's financial team to be available after a service two or three times a year, and on request at any time, to assist those who want to fill in a standing order or covenant form but lack the confidence to do so on their own.

Our giving should be proportionate

When Paul advised the Corinthians to budget their giving, he stressed it should be 'in keeping' with their income (1 Cor. 16:2). He emphasised that giving should be according to their means, rather than a fixed sum from everyone (2 Cor. 8:11). God will not disapprove of those who are unable to give large amounts, because our gifts are acceptable according to what we have, not according to what we don't have (2 Cor. 8:12).

So should we tithe – that is, give 10 per cent of our income? The New Testament never uses the word, even though the practice is warmly commended in the Old Testament (e.g. Mal. 3:10). What Paul encourages is giving that is voluntary and generous, planned and proportionate. He is at pains to avoid any sense of compulsion or legalism, which presumably explains why he avoids the 'T' word. For some, a tenth will be too much, and burdensome. For others, a tenth will be easily given, and, in all honesty, very much more than this could be released for the advance of the kingdom of God. If tithing is appropriate for you as an individual, that's great. But the New Testament never suggests that we should require a tenth as a standardised, obligatory, minimum or maximum sum.

Our giving will have mutual benefits

Paul recognises that circumstances change. Out of our plenty we are encouraged to give generously to those in need. Perhaps the day may come, he suggests, when they are enjoying plenty and will be able to supply our needs (2 Cor. 8:13–15). There is a mutuality in giving, for we store up a fund of goodwill which encourages us to grow ever more generous towards one another, not only in money, but in time, consideration and love.

What's more, the Corinthians' gifts will not only meet others' immediate needs, but the recipients will also enjoy spiritual benefits as a result, as their gratefulness turns into thankfulness to God. This praise will naturally be accompanied by prayers that seek God's blessing upon those whose financial support has been so timely (2 Cor. 9:12–14). In short, when we give money it can set in motion a mutually reinforcing cycle of spiritual blessing: the recipients benefit and praise God, and the donors benefit from the recipients' prayers. The positive power of giving can bring mutual spiritual enrichment.

So what about prosperity teaching? After all, Paul clearly says that when we sow sparingly we will reap sparingly, but when we sow generously we will reap generously (2 Cor. 9:6–11). The Bible is certainly not against material prosperity and wealth creation. We are, however, always encouraged to use our wealth wisely and to make sure the poor are provided for. The blessing of God can include prospering us materially, but cannot be restricted to an improvement in our personal finances. God's blessing in the present is all-encompassing, spiritual and relational, emotional and intellectual as well as material: every aspect of life can become an arena of God's favour upon us. And the fullness of God's blessing is beyond this life, in the abundance of heaven where, so far as I can see, material prosperity is a thing of the past. We can therefore affirm that while God is perfectly capable of blessing us with material prosperity, this is by no means the only or the necessary expression of his favour upon our lives.

When Paul presents this sowing and reaping principle to the Corinthians, his primary aim is to encourage their generosity. In our extremely materialistic world, where people are obsessed with money and selfish gain, we need to ensure that people are giving in

the way Paul commended. Not for some kind of supposedly automatic personal gain, but in response to a need and inspired by the
generosity of God in Christ. Paul is certainly not introducing them
to a previously unknown 'get rich quick' scheme, in which all they
have to do is send 100 gold pieces to Paul, and God will send them
1,000 by return. Any fund-raising programme that claims to
guarantee personal wealth if you make a generous contribution to
their cause is a woeful, even scandalous misrepresentation of Paul's
teaching. God will certainly look after us, and that may well include
a measure of financial provision, but his blessing cannot be automatically quantified in monetary terms. The favour of God is
concerned with the whole of life, and not narrowly with our bank
balance.

Above all, prosperity teaching that suggests material wealth is
the direct, automatic and universal consequence of godly living
has enormous problems with the New Testament. In the case of
Jesus Christ, no one has ever lived more generously, but he died at
a premature age, apparently owning only the clothes in which he
was arrested. Here is a life devoted to God's service in which God's
favour certainly did not find expression in long life or abundant
wealth. Paul's Corinthian correspondence debunks this fanciful
misinterpretation of the sowing and reaping principle in chapter 9.
Paul is commending to the Corinthians a generous lifestyle, but
what has been the impact in his own life of living for Christ? He
has no testimony of miraculous personal wealth or the first-century
equivalent of fast cars, expensive apartments and Armani suits. On
the contrary, the material consequence of Paul's discipleship has
been persecution, hardship, loss of reputation and frequent threats
of execution. He considers himself rich in the blessing of God, but
his life is manifestly not one of unhindered triumphant advance
and immense personal wealth. One disaster after another would be
a more accurate description:

I have worked much harder, been in prison more frequently,
been flogged more severely, and been exposed to death again
and again. Five times I received from the Jews the forty lashes
minus one. Three times I was beaten with rods, once I was
stoned, three times I was shipwrecked, I spent a night and a day

in the open sea, I have been constantly on the move. I have been in danger from rivers, in danger from bandits, in danger from my own countrymen, in danger from Gentiles; in danger in the city, in danger in the country, in danger at sea; and in danger from false brothers. I have laboured and toiled and have often gone without sleep; I have known hunger and thirst and have often gone without food; I have been cold and naked. Besides everything else, I face daily the pressure of my concern for all the churches. Who is weak, and I do not feel weak? Who is led into sin, and I do not inwardly burn? (2 Cor. 11:23–9)

Faced with the immediate context of 2 Corinthians, prosperity teaching is forced to one of two conclusions. Either the prosperity theory didn't work for Paul, in which case it can no longer be promulgated as a universal principle. Or the theory *does* work, and Paul didn't enjoy prosperity because he failed to sow with sufficient generosity – but such a judgement on the apostle's life can only be called absurd. In fact, of course, the hard evidence of Paul's own experiences demands a more subtle interpretation of his own teaching on sowing and reaping than that offered by the narrow materialism of the prosperity teachers. God has indeed promised that we will be able to reap generously of his blessing whenever we sow generously, and at times God's blessing may well be material and financial. But the totality of the blessing of God is on a much broader canvas. Christians who seek to live generously for the sake of personal material gain have completely missed the point. Personal material prosperity for every Christian is nowhere guaranteed in the New Testament. The essential motivation for living generously is that we serve an immeasurably generous Saviour, and enjoy the remarkable privileges of the favour of God.

Our giving needs to come from the heart

Paul and his team were not only inspired by the spontaneous generosity of the Macedonian Christians, they were also taught a lesson about giving. Once the Macedonians had prevailed upon them for an opportunity to contribute to the international offering, the missionary team expected them simply to hand over some money. That's only natural. We still tend to think of an offering as being about money, coins, notes and cheques. However, the Macedonians had a deeper understanding, and so, Paul explains, they did not do as expected and simply hand over some cash. Instead, they first gave themselves to the Lord (2 Cor. 8:5). It's as if they climbed onto an offering plate in person, taking all their personal belongings with them.

We can give a limited, or even a generous, offering of money to God, ask him to bless its use, and then treat the rest of our lives and possessions as if they were nothing to do with God. To give ourselves to God first is doubly dangerous. He may ask us for a larger sum of money than we had previously intended to give. He may take us seriously and lay claim to all our worldly wealth, so that all that we have can be used in his service. He may allow us to retain much, but now we will be looking after it for the Lord instead of keeping our wealth for ourselves. Once we begin to follow the Macedonian example, all that we have and all that we are belong to the Lord. Now that's the beginning of a truly, even dangerously, generous lifestyle!

Towards the end of this section of his letter, Paul explains that our giving needs to be neither reluctant, nor under compulsion, but 'cheerful' (2 Cor. 9:7). The Greek word Paul used is the root of the English word 'hilarious'. Today, those who win on the horses are sometimes said to be 'laughing all the way to the bank'. Paul dares to suggest that Christians can end up laughing all the way to the offering, delighted with the sheer privilege of giving our money away. This incredible reversal of normal human instincts can only make sense because of the extravagant generosity of God.

Paul ends his teaching on giving with a spontaneous celebration of God's 'indescribable gift', that is, the sacrifice of Jesus Christ (2 Cor. 9:15). If God never blessed us again, in any personal, tangible and immediate way, his giving would already have immeasurably surpassed the best of our generosity, in the extravagance of sending his Son to die in our place. Our giving is an expression of whole-life discipleship. We give in thankfulness. We give to relieve suffering. We give to maximise the strategic impact and advance of the gospel in this generation. And we can give in the joyous confidence that it is utterly impossible for his disciples ever to out-give the crucified God.

Chapter 14

Time for a New You

Colossians 3:1–10, 12–14

WHENEVER A MAJOR work of art is restored, controversy is sure to follow. Some critics will acclaim the work of the restorers, while others denounce them as incompetents who have defaced a masterpiece. In Part One of this book we explored some of the implications of being made in the image of God, the extraordinarily rich potential that is integral to human existence. At the same time we faced the harsh reality that the image has been defaced. In the countless generations of the human race, like years of grime veiling the brushstrokes and colours of a great painting, sin has built upon sin. Still made in the image of God, our human potential is disfigured by countless expressions of selfishness.

The image of God, so tarnished by the history of human sin, has been made manifest again in Christ. The one who reveals definitively the character of God at the same time shows us what it means to be truly human. In Christ the potential of being made in the image of God is unlocked. Discipleship means following Christ and seeking to become more like him. The more we are able to conform to Christ, the more the image of God is renewed within us. The greatest restoration work on planet Earth is not to be found on the walls of art galleries, but in the hearts of Christian believers. Whole-life discipleship means living in submission to Christ, the great Restorer, who is working to renew the image of God in every believer's life.

This new life begins with a death and resurrection. Paul explains that when we came to faith we died to the basic principles of this world and were raised to newness of life in Christ (Col. 2:20; 3:1).

Unlike the superficial legalism that was attracting the Colossians but was guaranteed to fail in the end, Paul saw death and resurrection into Christ as the only way to lay hold of opportunities for real and lasting inner change.

Discipleship is a Christ-centred way of life. We died with Christ (Col. 2:20), we were raised with Christ (Col. 3:1), we live under the reign of Christ in heaven (Col. 3:1), and Christ is our life (Col. 3:4). Our present life of discipleship is shaped by the two great comings of Christ, the triumph of the cross and his glorious return. Paul emphasises that when Christ appears, we will appear with him in glory (Col. 3:4). The work of restoring the divine image that was made possible at the cross will be completed beyond this life, when sin is stripped away from us and we shall be renewed in the perfection of the divine image. In Christ our created and redeemed potential shall be eternally fulfilled.

Discipleship is also profoundly shaped by the experience of baptism. Paul's language deliberately echoes the experience of the first believers when they were baptised. The language of death and resurrection is enacted in the experience of immersion and being raised up out of the water. The practical necessity of taking off wet clothes and putting on dry ones is deliberately brought back to mind when Paul speaks of us having 'taken off your old self' and 'put on the new self' (Col. 3:9–10). Now he encourages baptised believers to clothe themselves with the character of Christ (Col. 3:12) – that is, to get dressed in newness of life.

The transformations of discipleship require active determination. Paul tells the Colossians to *set their hearts on things above* (Col. 3:1). They must choose to re-orient their affections to the ways of Christ and deliberately cultivate heavenly appetites. At the same time, they must *set their minds on things above* (Col. 3:2). Their focus, priorities, and way of seeing life must all be re-tuned around the centrality of Christ, and this involves the totality of their being, heart and mind. Like a new television that can receive all available channels but must first be tuned in, effective discipleship requires us to tune our hearts and minds into Christ. And then we must choose to stay tuned.

Paul spells out the kind of changes we need to pursue by listing qualities that should be eradicated. In Colossians 2 he had rejected legalism and false asceticism. Now he makes it plain that the equal and opposite excesses of licence and self-indulgence must also be excluded if we want to pursue the way of discipleship. There are many lists within the New Testament of the characteristics of the sinful heart, and none pretend to be exhaustive. To the Colossians, Paul emphasises ways in which we burn with desire (Col. 3:5) and ways in which we burn with hostility (Col. 3:8). The desires Paul lists are mainly sexual excesses – Christianity is not anti-sexuality, which is a gift of God in creation, but anti-lust, which is the distortion of our sexuality in destructive ways. The non-sexual desire with which we can burn is 'greed' – that is, the consuming pursuit of material things – which Paul singles out as 'idolatry', echoing Jesus' warning that we cannot serve God and Mammon (Matt. 6:24). As to burning with hostility, Paul cites not only rage but also gossip, lying and swearing. These are sins of speech and behaviour that break relationships and entrench us in warring camps. Exaggerations, false promises, misrepresentations and inflated claims of our own importance and our accomplishments are all encompassed in this list. Put together, the two lists speak of different kinds of powerful and destructive inner energy. Whether in lust or in anger we can lose self-control to the detriment of others. At the same time, we dehumanise ourselves as we become self-consumed by the passions of lust or anger. Many films and television soap operas are built around these behaviour patterns. Many sensational newspaper headlines revel in the consequences of extreme self-indulgence, broken reputations, terminated careers and wrecked relationships.

A striking parallel can be found in the Greek god Zeus, who frequently disguised himself as anything from a shower of gold to a swan, in order to fool women into allowing him close enough so that he could rape them. Such disgusting, dehumanising behaviour suggests that the more we indulge our sinful nature, the more we become like the mythical gods, made in our image, than the Creator God, whose image within us is disfigured by our selfish passions. Without dwelling upon judgement or savouring any lurid details, Paul reminds us that a life of self-indulgence has inescapable and eternal consequences, unless we turn to Christ in repentance and faith – 'Because of these, the wrath of God is coming' (Col. 3:6).

Christian transformation takes place in two time zones. At conversion, we die to the old way of life (Col. 3:3). And yet in the walk of discipleship we are called to a present-day putting to death of the destructive qualities that distinguish the sinful nature (Col. 3:5). We have already 'taken off' the old self (Col. 3:9), and yet we must now rid ourselves of sin – that is, purge these ways from our lives and give them no house room. The clear implication is that our inner change is both a crisis and a process, both a decisive event in our conversion and a continuing discipline of the walk of discipleship. The sinful nature has been dethroned within us, but not yet exterminated. It no longer dictates our lives so easily, but is still quite capable of getting back in the driving seat if we allow it. The more we live carelessly, failing to choose decisively the ways of Christ, the more likely it is that the sinful nature will usurp control of our lives once again.

Paul sums up with precision this combination of past and present, active choice, and yet dependence upon God that marks the experience of conversion and the journey of discipleship: '[You] have put on the new self' – a once-for-all past event, an active choice, '. . . which is being renewed' – a continuing process, in the present, depending upon God (Col. 3:10).

Made in the image of God and yet suffering from a defaced image, the glorious truth is that God's image within us is being restored in Christ. The more we become like Christ, the more the image of God is recovered, the more wholeness we can enjoy, and the more fully we are able to become our true selves in Christ. We saw in Part One of this book that the image of God is multi-faceted – reason, creativity, moral awareness, spirituality, appreciation of beauty, relational beings able to give and receive love. All that we were designed for in creation becomes newly possible in Christ. Whole-life discipleship means fulfilling the potential the Creator originally set in our lives.

Time to get dressed

Disciples need to clothe themselves in newness of life. Salvation is God's gift, not something we can earn. But once we have been saved there are many active decisions to take, many priorities to change. The two lists of destructive desires that we looked at earlier in this chapter describe what life begins to look like when we do what comes naturally. Paul provided two lists for the Galatians, the works of the flesh and the fruit of the Spirit (Gal. 5:19–23). Even so, the Colossians are also given paired lists of vices and virtues. Just as the various lusts and hostilities destroy relationships, Paul gives us a contrasting list of five qualities that can only make our relationships better (Col. 3:12).

The first virtue is compassion

This speaks of a heart of pity, a deep yearning to make a positive difference in someone else's life. It's not enough, of course, to feel for others; true compassion will result in action. We see compassion at work repeatedly in Jesus' life. His heartfelt response to people's needs is apparent not only in his healing and deliverance ministry, but also in his preaching. Practical help for friends in need, social action and evangelism all flow from a heart stirred by compassion.

The second virtue is kindness

As we grow in kindness we learn to become more considerate, appreciative and willing to put ourselves out for the sake of others. We make time for others, rather than being entirely absorbed with our own needs. God's kindness, the extravagance of his generous love, is a common theme of the New Testament (Rom. 2:4, 11:22; Eph. 2:7; Titus 3:4). The more we grasp the Father's kindness towards us, the more we are called to express kindness to others.

The third virtue is humility

Paul had denounced the manipulative, false humility of the Colossian cult of angels (Col. 2:18, 23). True humility means lowliness, a healthy lack of inflated self-importance. Where true humility has taken root, there will be no haughtiness or love of show. We will be surprised at any fuss or attention and gladly waive our rights to any kind of special arrangements. Instead of getting upset that we are not on the front row of the platform or in the best seats of the house, we will be content with whatever is provided. We won't throw our weight around or become over-bearing towards our subordinates. We will become more concerned to meet the needs of others than be fussed over ourselves. The way of humility is the way of the incarnation and cross, for no one has ever given up so much for others, so graciously, as the Son of God (see Phil. 2:6–11 for a glorious song of the self-humbling descent of Christ).

The fourth virtue is gentleness

Christ demonstrated gentleness in his trial, when he refused to become aggressive, assertive or self-vindicating. There is also much gentleness in the way he deals with damaged people, never crushing them as he invited them to discover the love of God. Paul was not by nature a gentle man. Before his conversion, he was convinced he was serving God by imprisoning Christians and sanctioning their execution. Paul learnt well the imitation of Christ and so he urged the Philippians to let their gentleness be evident to all (Phil. 4:5). I preached once on that theme and a retired senior executive confessed that the words had cut him to the quick. He explained that he had always kept his staff under his thumb. He had been pushy and domineering, and now he realised that such attitudes brought dishonour to the name of Christ. As he reflected on his lack of gentleness, he realised why he had been such a hard task-master: 'I was afraid of them, fearing that one of them might outshine me and take my job. And so, to protect myself, I kept them down.' The more secure we are in Christ, the more able we are to take the risk of gentleness towards others.

The fifth virtue is patience

Too many people suffer from hidden rages and stored up grievances, keeping a record of wrongs. Some nurse a desire for revenge for many years. They refuse to let time dim the wrongs that others have done them. Being short-tempered is an all too familiar problem, which suggests that we could usefully define patience as being 'long-tempered'. Some of those in higher positions are impatient with junior staff, or with manual workers including railway staff, dustmen and shop workers. They treat them as less than fully human, as if the railway worker had put leaves on the line personally, or the cashier had arrived at work early in order to bruise every banana one by one. Others are impatient in the privacy of their own home, taking out their frustrations with life on their partner or children. When life gets too stressful those closest to us often become our lightning conductors. The gift of patience defuses any tendency to explode from time to time.

These virtues are very practical. Their expression is more likely to be appreciated than to cause a sensation. They are not spectacular or headline making, but if every professing Christian made it a priority to live in this way, the world would quickly begin to be a better place. So it makes good sense to examine ourselves and see whether one of these virtues has gone absent without leave from our lives. Is there any particular way in which you find it easy to drift from Christ's priorities and forget to be clothed in his virtues?

As we learn to clothe ourselves in these virtues, the local church has the potential to become a place of renewed and life-giving relationships. Paul urges us to bear with one another, which means we will sometimes become almost unbearable, and also to forgive one another, which means we will sometimes need to be forgiven (Col. 3:13). This is an act of will: we bear with one another and forgive one another not because we happen to feel like it, but because we choose to, in order to express the character of Christ. Paul sums up this crucial principle of keeping our relationships healthy by reminding us of our own experience of forgiveness: 'Forgive as the Lord forgave you' (Col. 3:13). When others let us down and need to be forgiven, we need to keep a sense of proportion: *we* have let God down so badly and need forgiving so very much. The forgiving power of Christ can then become our inspiration and also our resource: we forgive even as we are forgiven.

Christians are sometimes tempted to berate and condemn the Church, but we are surely without excuse. There are no doubt parts of the Church that we could not possibly join, because we would feel like a fish out of water. But we must love the Church because Christ loves the Church. And we must forgive the Church, whether as an organisation or individuals within it, for the simple but profound reason that Christ has forgiven us.

Paul adds a sixth virtue to this list, which comes as no surprise. Continuing with the picture of getting dressed, he urges us to clothe ourselves with love as an outer garment which holds everything together in perfect unity (Col. 3:14). Fashions change, and we don't have an outer garment in the modern world that performs this function. Some find it helpful to think of love like a large, heavy overcoat, warm and comforting even in the bleakest mid-winter.

The pre-eminence of love is a common New Testament theme (e.g. 1 Cor. 13; Gal. 5:6). When Jesus summed up the Old Testament law, he called us to love God with our whole being and love our neighbours as ourselves (Matt. 22:37–40). His additional law of love calls us even deeper into expressing the character of God: to love one another as Christ has loved us (John 13:34–5). Love gives motive and meaning to the other virtues. God's saving love for us is the inspiration and the driving force that quickens us to a lifestyle of self-giving love.

It would be possible to live a virtuous life on a desert island, but it would be very limited. The crowning virtues of the Christian life, so gloriously descriptive of the character of Jesus Christ, can only find adequate expression in the company of others. For whole-life discipleship to be fully experienced, we need one another. The appeal to put on the 'overcoat' of love comes not just to an isolated individual, but to the Church: we need to clothe ourselves in love together!

The invitation of the New Testament is plain: it's not only time for a new you, it's time for a new us. Christ has made it possible for us to be clothed in his virtues and experience the image of God being restored in our lives. Why settle for sectarianism, self-centredness, arrogance, party spirit, taking offence easily and a disposition given to negativity, when our inheritance in Christ allows us to be clothed in compassion, kindness, humility, gentleness, patience and love. All too often Christians clothe themselves in the rags of selfishness and self-righteousness when we have become entitled to wear virtues fit for the King! Please don't settle for religious rags, when your life can begin to be reclothed in the riches of the character of Christ.

Chapter 15

Love Among Equals

Colossians 3:11–4:1

EVERY SOCIETY HAS its winners and losers, the people who are admired and the people about whom jokes are told. The British have a stockpile of jokes about the Irish, the Americans have the Poles, the Scandinavians have one another. Jewish men turned this sense of a confident social hierarchy into a prayer, thanking God daily that they were born a Jew, not a Gentile; free, not a slave; a man, not a woman. Once they realised that Christ had died for all people and that, as a direct result, the Holy Spirit is being poured out upon all believers, the New Testament writers soon got to work on dismantling the first Christians' inner walls of prejudice. When Paul called the Colossians to express the life of Christ, putting on his virtues and above all his self-giving love, the social divisions of the Roman world were blown apart: 'Here there is no Greek or Jew, circumcised or uncircumcised, barbarian, Scythian, slave or free, but Christ is all, and is in all' (Col. 3:11).

'No Greek or Jew' speaks of national divisions. We would perhaps say American or Russian, British or French, or in these days of a new National Assembly, Scottish or English. 'No circumcised or uncircumcised' speaks of religious divisions linked to ethnic origin. 'Slave or free' speaks of social divisions and class consciousness. 'No barbarian' speaks of the Gentile world beyond the borders of the Roman Empire, which was considered uneducated, uncivilised and culturally inferior. 'No Scythian' speaks of the tribes who came from around the Black Sea, who were famous for producing many of the toughest slaves. They were described by Josephus, the renowned Jewish historian, as 'little better than wild beasts'. Everyone considered them to be ethnically and intellectually the lowest of the low. In more recent times this has been the attitude towards gypsies in much of Europe, or perhaps the hillbillies in America. In his letter to the Galatians, Paul's summary of the defunct divisions is more succinct and emphatically includes the gender division – no male nor female (Gal. 3:28).

In these few words Paul encapsulates the major social divisions of the ancient world. His affirmation is revolutionary: in the Church, there is no place for any of them. No matter how deeply these divisions have shaped people's lives before they came to faith, they have been superseded and abolished. There is no place or excuse for Christians to parade their old prejudices. By faith in Christ we have joined a new society and enjoy an irreversible equality. Paul explains this in two related ways. *Christ is all* – that is, what we need for salvation is found in Christ, and we bring no merits from our particular social and ethnic origin. And *Christ is in all* – that is, by the Holy Spirit the risen Christ indwells every believer, irrespective of our ethnic and social origins, endowing every single believer with the same high standing as an adopted child of God.

This marks more than the abolition of racist, sexist and religious bigotry. It also leaves neither place nor excuse for instinctive prejudice and institutional discrimination. This is crucial. The gospel not only excludes overt attitudes that dehumanise others or make them less significant than ourselves; it also calls us to a rigorous self-examination, seeking to eradicate all such attitudes from our minds and hearts as soon as they surface. We need to come to terms with how deeply many of us are conditioned to embrace automatically a set of prejudices that the gospel makes indefensible.

The New Testament principle is liberating and exhilarating. It seems astonishing to read such enlightened words in a document 2,000 years old. But the history of the Church has often been much less encouraging. Churches have all too easily become bastions of social, racial and sexual hierarchy. That is greatly to our shame, but the invitation of the New Testament is undimmed. We need to learn how to abandon our hierarchies and prejudices and take the risk of embracing the radical equality of new life in Christ. When we experience this new equality in action, it is extraordinarily inspiring and rewarding.

Time bomb under slavery

One of the most remarkable New Testament documents is so short that it is easily overlooked, Paul's letter to Philemon. This letter and the main letter to the Colossians were carried by Tychicus, who was serving as Paul's personal postman (Col. 4:7). The church at Colosse met in the house of Philemon and Apphia, who had a son, Archippus, who was also a believer (Philem. 1–2). Tychicus did not travel to Colosse alone, but was accompanied by Onesimus (Col. 4:9; Philem. 12).

Onesimus had been Philemon's slave. His name meant 'useful', but Paul acknowledges that he had previously been useless to his master (Philem. 11). He had run away (Philem. 12), and may have robbed his master (Philem. 18). Perhaps Onesimus thought his luck had run out when he met Paul in prison, but in fact he was converted under Paul's ministry (Philem. 10). He then demonstrated that his new faith was genuine by becoming very helpful to Paul in prison (Philem. 12–13).

Paul is now returning Onesimus to his master. Roman law was very clear about the rights of slave owners in such circumstances. At the very least they were expected to punish runaways severely, and were even entitled to have them executed. Paul is therefore taking a risk with Onesimus' life in insisting that he must abide by the law. His letter to Philemon is an appeal for mercy for his repentant and converted slave.

Paul gives no direct repudiation of slavery in his letters. It was integral to the Empire's social structures, and an explicit attack on slavery would very probably have led to the suppression of Christianity as a political, anti-Roman ideology. But Paul's letter goes much further than an appeal for mercy. His radical Christian values are profoundly subversive of the status quo because he is convinced that brotherhood in Christ means equality in Christ. This innocent-looking letter to Philemon sets a time bomb ticking under the institution of slavery.

Paul urges Philemon to receive Onesimus back into his home, not merely with mercy but 'no longer as a slave, but . . . as a dear brother' (Philem. 16). He describes Onesimus as 'my very heart' (Philem. 12) and as 'very dear to me' (Philem. 16), and then he adds that Onesimus will now be even more dear to Philemon, 'both as a man and as a brother in the Lord' (Philem. 16). Paul makes a comparison between master and slave, affirming that Onesimus took Philemon's place in being so helpful to the apostle (Philem. 13). He also compares the returning slave with himself, asking Philemon to 'welcome him as you would welcome me' (Philem. 17). In normal circumstances, a runaway slave would be treated to the worst possible conditions, whereas Philemon would presumably have the best bedroom prepared when expecting a visit from the apostle Paul. To cap it all, Paul not only expects obedience from Philemon in these matters, he even states his confidence that Philemon 'will do even more than I ask' (Philem. 21).

The only way to interpret such instructions is that the letter to Philemon is the most astonishingly subversive tract. If Philemon took the implications of Paul's letter seriously, we have to wonder whether anything would be left of the familiar and traditional relationship of master and slave. Once you welcome the slave as a dear brother, with the same welcome given to the apostle, he is very close to being no longer a slave at all.

Discipleship at home and work

The early Christians were living out their faith within the strict and automatic hierarchies of Gentile and Jewish society within the Roman Empire. And so the question inevitably arose, if we enjoy a new equality in Christ, what does that mean for the key relationships around which daily life is built. Several New Testament letters contain 'household codes' – that is, practical guidance for relationships between husbands and wives, parents and children, slave owners and slaves. There are many similarities between the household codes in Colossians and Ephesians, although the latter has more detail, and so we will refer to both as we explore the practical implications for our relationships of this new way of living.

Slaves are called to unreserved obedience. They are encouraged to develop a servant heart, working hard whether their master is present or absent. Inspiration for such dedication can be found in the fact that, ultimately, they are serving Christ himself (Col. 3:22–

4; Eph. 6:5–8). Meanwhile, slave owners are reminded that they share the same heavenly master with their slaves, and Christ shows no favouritism. They therefore need to provide what is 'right and fair' for their slaves (Col. 4:1). This combination of matching responsibilities can readily be extended into the modern workplace, where staff have a Christian duty to work well and bosses have an equivalent duty to treat their staff well, in terms of pay, conditions and attitudes.

Paul's letter to the Ephesians adds two telling requirements (Eph. 6:9). Christian masters are banned from threatening their slaves, and they are told to 'treat their slaves in the same way'. This refers back to the previous section of instructions to slaves in one of two ways. Either the masters must treat their slaves in the manner of Christ, who treats slaves and masters equally without any kind of discrimination. Or, just as the slaves must work as if they were serving the Lord, their masters must treat their slaves in the way Christ would treat a slave. In the era of legalised slavery, without any possibility of employment protection through legislation and unionisation, these instructions are quite remarkable. The slave owners are required to accept reciprocity, rather than calling all the shots as petty tyrants in their own homes.

Children are instructed to 'obey' their parents in everything, with the promise that this pleases the Lord (Col. 3:20). Once again, Ephesians provides a fuller picture by adding a quotation from the Ten Commandments (Eph. 6:1–3). This clarifies the instruction helpfully. While young children living in the parental home have a duty to obey, we have a lifelong duty to honour our parents. (I have explored this shift of emphasis and the transitions of young adulthood in *The Ten Commandments and the Decline of the West*.)

Just as with slaves and masters, there is a reciprocal obligation for parents and fathers – particularly the latter. Colossians warns fathers not to embitter their children, who will then become discouraged (Col. 3:21). Ephesians warns fathers not to exasperate their children (Eph. 6:4) – that is, 'wind them up' to a point of deep irritation or annoyance. Here the emphasis is upon abuse of power. While children are called to serve, Christian parents are required to rein in from the traditional absolutism that would be inclined to say, 'I am entitled to do anything I like in my own home.'

The absence of mention of mothers does not mean that mothers do not abuse power too. But it does seem to suggest that fathers are often particularly good at embittering or exasperating their children. What's more, the Ephesian parents are told to bring up their children 'in the training and instruction of the Lord' (Eph. 6:4). This is presented as an obligation for Christian fathers, not something they should leave entirely to a child's mother, as a kind of 'woman's work'. Our children learn about our faith not only through our words, but through our behaviour. If we say one thing but do another, they will spot the discrepancy every time.

The new approaches of Christian parenthood begin with a searching question: how does Jesus exercise authority in the Gospels? Parents need to learn from the Servant King. We bring up our children in the way of Christ, not with iron discipline, starving them of affection and encouragement, but with the grace, patience and kindness we have received from our Father in heaven. Parental tyrants have as little place in the kingdom of God as tyrants in the workplace.

Wives are called to submit to their husbands (Col. 3:18), as is fitting in the Lord (Eph. 5:22). Some commentators argue that this instruction simply inks over the conventional patriarchal marriage of the time. Others argue that the Christian distinctive is voluntary submission, since the women are being instructed to do something that would normally be automatic and imposed – with no options, choices or voluntarism. It is vital to notice the different verbs used. Wives submit, children obey, despite the traditional English wedding service. Here is something more subtle: Paul commends a willingness to give ground, but he doesn't countenance an unthinking, blind or craven obedience. Ephesians adds the instruction that a wife should respect her husband (Eph. 5:33). This carries with it two implicit warnings. First, a woman can become dismissive of her husband, treating him as no more than a 'big kid', perhaps not least in the way she talks about him in his absence. Second, a man's poor behaviour can put him in a position where he no longer deserves his wife's respect, so that if she does still respect him it is not according to his merits or rights, but thanks to her generosity of spirit.

The real shock comes with the instructions for husbands. We

are expressly told not to be harsh with our wives (Col. 3:19). This rules out traditional marital assaults in many societies: verbal attacks, physical abuse and aggressive demands for sexual favours. Such things are difficult to eradicate from society today, let alone in the deeply chauvinistic world of the first-century Empire. But Christian discipleship excludes normal macho behaviour. Husbands are also commanded to love their wives – that is, to retain tenderness, deep affection and the highest regard. There is no excuse for taking a wife for granted. Casual, dismissive and derogatory attitudes towards a wife, or indeed any woman, are totally unacceptable for a committed disciple of Christ.

Ephesians adds a further phrase which raises the stakes of love enormously for husbands: 'love your wives, just as Christ loved the church and gave himself up for her' (Eph. 5:25). Clearly, husbands cannot love their wives in every way that Christ loved the Church. They are not asked to die on a cross as an atoning sacrifice to secure salvation for their wives. The crucial comparison is that Christ's love is self-giving, not self-centred, and he put us so far before his own needs that he was willing to lay down his life. This is love to the utmost, love that is extravagant and totally self-sacrificing, love without a hint of selfishness. The love of the cross and male domination are like oil and water. They just cannot mix. The love of Christ is not about 'Where's my supper?' and 'The little woman at home' and 'Obey me, it will do you good'. The love of Christ is the most extraordinary miracle of servanthood in the history of the human race. And now Paul commands husbands to love in the way of the cross. This is awesome and revolutionary. Husbands who take the New Testament seriously should have on their lips not a command but a question. Instead of sitting on the throne of male domination, issuing our wives with a chauvinist decree – 'Submit to me!' – we should take the towel of a servant and ask our wives a question worthy of Christ – 'How can I serve you best?'

In each of these cases, Paul is looking for radical social change from above, not below. The powerful are invited to lay down their domination, rather than having it torn from them by an uprising of the weak. The reason for this approach is that he is reinterpreting our relationships in the light of the cross, where the Lord of the cosmos humbles himself to be the servant of all. Speaking to the weak in the Roman Empire, the slaves, children and wives, he encourages them not to stand up for their rights, but to choose to serve, just as Christ served in his trial and death. Speaking to the strong in the Empire, the slave owners, parents and husbands, just as Christ gave up the authority of heaven to serve us even to the cross, Paul encourages them to learn to respect and serve those whom, in the customs of the day, they had every right to tyrannise, dominate and rule over.

There is a revolutionary time bomb ticking in these words. Eventually Christians caught hold of the implications for slavery and took a strong lead in the abolitionist movement. It's not too late for Christians to begin to model new patterns of family life, between parents and children, and between husbands and wives, in which the servant love of Christ transforms the quality and character of our relationships so that our home life becomes a living demonstration of the transforming power of the cross. For that to happen, acute responsibility rests upon us all, but perhaps especially upon fathers and husbands who have been all too often inclined to ignore this radical redefinition of parental and marital responsibilities.

If the heart of the biblical understanding of marriage was hierarchy, men could claim that their aim was 'to keep their wives in their place'. But when the heart of being a Christian husband is the servant love of Christ, my great aim and ambition must become not to squash my wife, but to serve her, to give her what she needs instead of demanding what I need, and to burn with an ambition to see her potential in every aspect of life realised to the full. Nothing less than that high and noble ambition, which requires a total reversal of much patriarchal thinking, can give adequate expression to the New Testament command. Christ has served me to the utmost, and now I must make a lifelong journey of learning to serve my wife.

Ephesians sums up the distinctively Christian approach to every kind of relationship, at work, at home and at church: 'Submit to one another out of reverence to Christ' (Eph. 5:21). Here is an all-inclusive mutuality that will result in relationships being renewed and old hierarchies overturned, in the way of the cross. As workers and bosses, parents and children, husbands and wives, church leaders and church members, in every aspect of life we show reverence for Christ when we choose to serve. As I prefer your needs to my own, Christ is honoured. Whenever we throw our weight around or only think of ourselves, Christ is dishonoured. If only we are prepared to take the risk of putting New Testament values into practice within our local church, we can discover unbounded privileges of belonging and mutual support. Whole-life discipleship calls us to take daily risks of servanthood in the way of the cross. That's what love among equals is all about.

The 'one anothers' in the New Testament

Building on this principle of serving one another, the New Testament contains a large collection of 'one another' sayings. They are a remarkably demanding and exciting compilation of our responsibilities towards one another.

John 13:34
'A new command I give you: Love one another. As I have loved you, so you must love one another.'

John 13:35
'All men will know that you are my disciples if you love one another.'

Romans 12:10
'Be devoted to one another in brotherly love. Honour one another above yourselves.'

Romans 12:16
'Live in harmony with one another. Do not be proud, but be willing to associate with people of low position. Do not be conceited.'

Romans 13:8
'Let no debt remain outstanding, except the continuing debt to love one another, for he who loves his fellow-man has fulfilled the law.'

Romans 14:13
'Therefore let us stop passing judgment on one another. Instead, make up your mind not to put any stumbling-block or obstacle in your brother's way.'

Romans 15:7
'Accept one another, then, just as Christ accepted you, in order to bring praise to God.'

Romans 15:14
'I myself am convinced, my brothers, that you yourselves are full of goodness, complete in knowledge and competent to instruct one another.'

Romans 16:16
'Greet one another with a holy kiss. All the churches of Christ send greetings.'

1 Corinthians 1:10
'I appeal to you, brothers, in the name of our Lord Jesus Christ, that all of you agree with one another so that there may be no divisions among you and that you may be perfectly united in mind and thought.'

1 Corinthians 16:20
'All the brothers here send you greetings. Greet one another with a holy kiss.'

2 Corinthians 13:12
'Greet one another with a holy kiss.'

Galatians 5:13
'You, my brothers, were called to be free. But do not use your freedom to indulge the sinful nature; rather, serve one another in love.'

Ephesians 4:2
'Be completely humble and gentle; be patient, bearing with one another in love.'

Ephesians 4:32
'Be kind and compassionate to one another, forgiving each other, just as in Christ God forgave you.'

Ephesians 5:19
'Speak to one another with psalms, hymns and spiritual songs. Sing and make music in your heart to the Lord.'

Ephesians 5:21
'Submit to one another out of reverence for Christ.'

Colossians 3:13
'Bear with one another and forgive whatever grievances you may have against one another. Forgive as the Lord forgave you.'

Colossians 3:16
'Let the word of Christ dwell in you richly as you teach and admonish one another with all wisdom, and as you sing psalms, hymns and spiritual songs with gratitude in your hearts to God.'

1 Thessalonians 5:11
'Therefore encourage one another and build each other up, just as in fact you are doing.'

Titus 3:3
'At one time we too were foolish, disobedient, deceived and enslaved by all kinds of passions and pleasures. We lived in malice and envy, being hated and hating one another.'

Hebrews 3:13
'But encourage one another daily, as long as it is called Today, so that none of you may be hardened by sin's deceitfulness.'

Hebrews 10:24
'And let us consider how we may spur one another on towards love and good deeds.'

Hebrews 10:25
'Let us not give up meeting together, as some are in the habit of doing, but let us encourage one another – and all the more as you see the Day approaching.'

James 4:11
'Brothers, do not slander one another. Anyone who speaks against his brother or judges him speaks against the law and judges it. When you judge the law, you are not keeping it, but sitting in judgment on it.'

1 Peter 1:22
'Now that you have purified yourselves by obeying the truth so that you have sincere love for your brothers, love one another deeply, from the heart.'

1 Peter 3:8
'Finally, all of you, live in harmony with one another; be sympathetic, love as brothers, be compassionate and humble.'

1 Peter 4:9
'Offer hospitality to one another without grumbling.'

1 Peter 5:5
'Young men, in the same way be submissive to those who are older. Clothe yourselves with humility towards one another, because, "God opposes the proud but gives grace to the humble." '

1 Peter 5:14
'Greet one another with a kiss of love. Peace to all of you who are in Christ.'

1 John 1:7
'But if we walk in the light, as he is in the light, we have fellowship with one another, and the blood of Jesus, his Son, purifies us from all sin.'

1 John 3:11
'This is the message you heard from the beginning: We should love one another.'

1 John 3:23
'And this is his command: to believe in the name of his Son, Jesus Christ, and to love one another as he commanded us.'

1 John 4:7
'Dear friends, let us love one another, for love comes from God. Everyone who loves has been born of God and knows God.'

1 John 4:11
'Dear friends, since God so loved us, we also ought to love one another.'

1 John 4:12
'No-one has ever seen God; but if we love each other, God lives in us and his love is made complete in us.'

2 John 5
'And now, dear lady, I am not writing you a new command but one we have had from the beginning. I ask that we love one another.'

Chapter 16

The Disciple-Making Church

Colossians 4

WHEN PEOPLE HAVE their first counselling appointment, they often save their most important words till the last moment. They are about to leave the room when they pause and add, 'Oh, there's just one more thing . . .' Love letters can also save things up: not so much bad news as the most fulsome expressions of devoted love. Teenage love letters sometimes devote almost as much space to the PS, PPS, and PPPS as they do to the main letter. As to the letters in the New Testament, the last chapter is often the most difficult part for today's readers to get into, although the first audience must have been all ears, waiting to see who got a personal mention. Long lists of greetings to people we don't know seem distant and even tedious. But if we dig deeper, there are some great insights to discover for whole-life discipleship.

Devoted to prayer

Paul encourages the Colossians to 'devote' themselves to prayer (Col. 4:2). This means stick with prayer, keep at it, persevere. For those of us who sometimes find prayer difficult, it's helpful to discover that the first Christians often struggled as well. The moment we think about prayer, a hundred urgent tasks press upon us. When we begin praying, all at once we either fall asleep or our mind gets sidetracked into thinking about other things.

The Jews addressed wandering mind trouble by having fixed hours and set patterns for prayer. The first Christian approach to prayer was spontaneous and yet continuous. They were no doubt inspired by the fact that Jesus had an open line to the Father at all times. He spent time alone in prayer but wherever he was he continued to be tuned into the Father's presence. Our risk is often either to have a set time of prayer that loses all freshness and vitality, or to stress spontaneity and then find it difficult to get round to prayer at all. In a world that is moving faster and faster where we feel pressured to live from day to day without reference to God, the typical complaint of many Christians is that we find ourselves overworked and under-prayed. We need to recover an in-depth spirituality where we learn to make new connections between prayer and every part of life. From the traffic jam to the checkout queue, there is nowhere that we cannot commune with the living God. In every waking moment, the Father makes himself available to every follower of Christ.

Paul commends two qualities in prayer, 'being watchful and thankful' (Col. 4:2). Watchful means 'stay alert!' We need to keep guard over ourselves to avoid drowsiness in prayer and distractions in life, keeping focused on the priority of following Jesus. We also need a sense of watchfulness on behalf of our society, making time to pray together about issues that could drag our nation further from the values of God or to create new opportunities for the gospel. There are times when watchfulness is just between us and God. At other times, we will be praying with a Bible in one hand and a newspaper in the other, or praying while watching the news on TV.

We have already explored the theme of thankfulness which runs through this letter from beginning to end (Col. 1:12; 2:7; 3:15, 17; 4:2). By returning to this key-word, Paul reminds the Colossians of the discipline of thankfulness. We need to make sure we don't take the good things in life for granted, but instead cultivate an appreciative attitude of heart. Recently I was speaking at a house party where Susie was converted. When she understood the gospel for the first time her eyes lit up. 'This is absolutely wonderful,' she said. 'But why aren't Christians more excited about it?' The discipline of thankfulness keeps us grateful for the cross of Christ. The more we express thankfulness to God, the more others will find us encouraging and supportive. Appreciative disciples not only express their glad thankfulness to God, but also help one another to thrive and so fulfil our potential in Christ.

An open door for witness

To the general encouragement to keep praying, Paul adds a personal request. Not for his release from prison nor that he would be spared the threat of martyrdom. Nor for his immediate, daily needs in difficult circumstances. These would be natural ways for many of us to request prayer support in Paul's position. But he has his eyes on a much more important goal; and so he asks the Colossians to pray for 'an open door for our message' (Col. 4:3) and the ability to proclaim it clearly, as he should (Col. 4:4). Even in prison, Paul's first concern is evangelism and the advance of the gospel. In fact, he was exceptionally resourceful, making sure he seized every opportunity for witness. He explained to the Philippians that as a result of his house arrest, everyone in the palace guard had heard the gospel (Phil. 1:13). It seems that one or two soldiers were chained to Paul every day, and so he made sure that no day was complete without his captive audience hearing about his personal saving faith in Jesus Christ.

In the light of Paul's requests, a church's prayer life needs to include enthusiastic support for world mission. If a church has sent Christians overseas, they need to be prayed for regularly. If none have been sent directly, we need to pray for Christian organisations working around the world, and also that God will soon give us the privilege of being a sending church once again.

The 'open door for our message' that speaks of world mission also highlights our own responsibility for personal witness. Paul encourages the Colossians to be wise in the way they behave with outsiders, urging them to make the most of every opportunity (Col. 4:5). This certainly doesn't require us to buttonhole every passing pagan, and it's no excuse to become an evangelistic bore at home or work, incapable of joining in any conversation without turning it into an evangelistic blitzkrieg. On the other hand, we equally have no excuse to become a secret Christian, always avoiding any mention of our faith. As we pray for world mission, we need also to pray that a door will open for personal witnessing opportunities and that we will know how to use them wisely.

Paul identifies the best recipe for every disciple's style of conversation – 'full of grace, seasoned with salt' (Col. 4:6). No salt at all and our conversation will be bland, with the 'niceness' of the kind of well-meaning Christian who never stands up for anything. Too much and our conversation will become unpalatable, with the result that others will avoid our company just as they would avoid over-salted food. There have been times in my life when I have tended towards each of these extremes, too busy blending in to speak up for Christ and his kingdom, or too abrasive to be heard. No salt and too much salt both have the same result: we end up putting people off Christ rather than attracting them towards him. To be full of grace is to carry something of the attractiveness of Jesus, his mercy, patience and love. To be seasoned with salt means that people will know where we stand on the gospel and biblical morality. The Pharisees were great at expressing salt without grace. The disciple of Christ is called to imitate and express the Master's combination of an uncompromising willingness to speak out for truth and goodness in a broad context of generosity, kindness and grace.

Friends in Christ

The greetings in Paul's letters reveal an enormous capacity for friendship. He is not afraid to tell people how much he admires them. He expresses his appreciation in public, to whole churches; and he is happy to tell people that he is praying for them. In all these ways, British reserve can hold us back from full discipleship expressed in free and easy relationships. Sometimes we are so inhibited about expressing appreciation that we only speak out words of encouragement and affection when someone is about to move away. On church weekends I sometimes invite everyone present to send at least one card of thanks to another person in the church, whose contribution they have admired without so far getting round to letting them know. We have to unlock the flood-gates and release a great tidal wave of positive and supportive words of appreciation within the family of God.

It seems amazing to think that, until the last ten or twenty years, many churches never had coffee after services. After the closing prayer, some congregations practically raced for the door, escaping back to the privacy of their own home without saying anything more than 'Lovely sermon, Vicar!' Some churches never had a meal together, or only a rather formal special event, until they started doing Alpha courses. Although it's only by personal faith that we become believers, discipleship is a lifestyle that is best not practised alone. The more we invest in loving relationships as God's people together, the more we are able to thrive in the service of Christ.

Paul was also willing to give public expression to his own vulnerability. He described the only Jews among his fellow workers as a great comfort (Col. 4:11), which gives a hint of the emotional cost to a Jew of working to establish churches among foreigners for most of his life. He valued the personal support of people from a similar background, who could supply the consolation of friend-ship and prayer as he faced the prospect of death. We, too, need the support of personal friends as well as a sense of belonging that should ideally encompass everyone in our local church.

Paul also requests that the Colossians will 'remember' his chains (Col. 4:18). The shadow of the cross is a hallmark of authentic Christian living, for leaders and for every disciple. Jesus forewarned us to expect hostility and persecution, since the world is bound to treat his disciples in the way it treated him (John 15:20). Paul advised Timothy that 'everyone who wants to live a godly life will be persecuted' (2 Tim. 3:12). He told the Philippians that he wanted to know Christ not only in the power of his cross but also in the fellowship of his sufferings (Phil. 3:10). After the first apostles had been flogged on the orders of the Sanhedrin, they were 'rejoicing because they had been counted worthy of suffering disgrace for the Name' (Acts 5:41). The persecution of disciples is an inevit-ability and yet somehow a privilege, in the way of the cross. The fellowship of his disciples is the fellowship of the crucified.

Despite this inevitability and privilege, in the request to 'remem-ber' his chains, Paul acknowledges his need for comfort, support and prayer in his hour of danger. Some measure of persecution may be unavoidable, but we still need one another's support when life gets tough. Although Christ was desperately alone at the cross, we have the privilege of supporting one another. I have often come across hospital wards where the other patients are amazed to see how many visitors gather around the bed of a Christian. In times of trouble, true disciples are called to be faithful friends.

Mature and fully assured

Epaphras had visited Paul in prison. He seems to have come from Colosse originally (Col. 4:12) and had planted the Colossian church (Col. 1:7). He brought to Paul a report of how things were going, both the good things about the church and the infiltration of false teaching. Presumably the visit was not only to seek Paul's advice, but also to give the apostle his personal support and encouragement. Unfortunately, Epaphras' visit became unexpectedly prolonged when the Roman authorities decided to make him Paul's fellow prisoner (Philem. 23). The poor chap's pastoral visit had unexpected and prolonged results!

Paul pays tribute to the Colossians' leader in chains, by telling them of Epaphras' hard work, always wrestling – literally agonising – in prayer for the three churches of the Lycus valley (Col. 4:12). Once again we see the early Christians not easily swayed or disheartened by unexpected and difficult circumstances. Stickability and resolve were their hallmarks as they followed in the way of the cross. In the same way that Jesus set his face to Jerusalem, walking towards his death, we need to set our faces when life gets tough, choosing to live for Jesus according to the ways of Jesus.

Epaphras' prayer for the Colossian church gives an excellent summary of Paul's teaching on discipleship: '. . . that you may stand firm in all the will of God, mature and fully assured' (Col. 4:12). The exotic and legalistic extras with which they have been toying will never be able to deliver the full assurance they seek. They will be mature – that is, complete or perfected – not through the distractions and novelties of asceticism, speculation or ecstatic super-spirituality – however impressive these things may appear at first glance – but through a full-blown dependence upon Christ. They need to be fully convinced of the gospel and receive in full measure all that God has stored up for them in Christ. And they need to put their new life into practice, as they clothe themselves with the character of Christ and learn to give and receive love among equals, at home, at work and as a local church. We need to know and to show the good news. That's the fullness of whole-life discipleship.

The false discipleship of the infiltrators made genuine Christians feel insecure and second-best. True discipleship helps believers to grow in confidence that fullness is found in Christ and we have access to all the spiritual resources we need by faith in him. Just as Paul seeks to give renewed assurance to the Colossian Christians, helping them to fulfil their potential in Christ, he expects them to do the same for one another. Discipleship finds its fulfilment not in an isolated believer, however dedicated, but in Christians who are seeking to express the life of Christ in God's new family of love. Disciples need to come together to work out how to become an effective disciple-making church. We are called to make new disciples who are coming to faith for the first time, and also to help one another to continue to journey deeper into discipleship.

No matter how much we have entered into the love of the Father, no matter how much his Spirit has been at work in our lives restoring the divine image, no matter how much we have put into practice the positive holiness of Christ, in the way of the cross and self-giving love, there is always so much more to discover. The risen Christ still speaks the same words of invitation, not only to new converts who are just coming to faith, but also to those who have been disciples for several, or even many, years – 'Come, follow me.' In the glorious adventure of whole-life discipleship, all of us have only just begun.

Selected Further Reading

Out of the many books that would be listed in a full bibliography, here are just a few that are unmissable.

Classics
Augustine, *Confessions*
John Bunyan, *Pilgrim's Progress*
John Wesley, *Journals*

Recent Books
Dietrich Bonhoeffer, *Life Together* (SCM, 1954)
Richard Foster, *Streams of Living Water* (Collins, 1999)
Donald Kraybill, *The Upside Down Kingdom* (Herald Press, 1978)
Gordon MacDonald, *Ordering Your Private World* (Moody Press, 1984)
J. I. Packer, *Knowing God* (Hodder, 1973)
John Stott, *The Cross of Christ* (IVP, 1986)
John Stott, *Issues Facing Christians Today* (Collins, 1990)
John Stott, *The Contemporary Christian* (IVP, 1992)
David Watson, *Discipleship* (Hodder, 1981)

The most important reading matter for any disciple of Christ is the Bible. While all Christians need to be encouraged to read Christian books, above all we need to get to know the Bible better. And that means making the time and effort to read it, often and well!

Further Resources

1 Discussion starters are available for each chapter of *I Believe in Discipleship*. You can obtain these from 'Kairos – Church from Scratch'. *Website*: www.kairos.org.uk

2 Tapes of Rob Warner's preaching on the themes of each chapter are also available, together with a wide range of his other teaching. Details are available from Kairos.

3 Rob Warner's other books develop many of the key themes of *I Believe in Discipleship*. They are available from all good bookshops:

21st Century Church (Hodder & Stoughton, 1994, revised edition, Kingsway, 1999)
Alive in the Spirit (Hodder & Stoughton, 1997)
Baptism and You (Kingsway, 2000)
Praying with Jesus (Hodder & Stoughton, 1999)
Prepare for Revival (Hodder & Stoughton, 1995)
The Sermon on the Mount (Kingsway, 1998)
The Ten Commandments and the Decline of the West (Kingsway, 1997)
Walking with God (Hodder & Stoughton, 1998)

Also in this series:

I Believe in Heaven on Earth

Life after life for humanity and planet earth

Tony and Patricia Higton

As the millennium dawns there is much speculation about the big questions: how long can life on earth, as we know it, survive? What will happen to the human race and planet earth? Is there life after death for the individual? Is Jesus coming back?

Tony and Patricia Higton explain in straightforward terms that many biblical prophecies have come true, giving credibility to those which address the big questions about the future. They do not avoid controversy, but suggest a way forward for Christians to agree on the major issues, striking a balance between 'doom and boom'. This fascinating book is an eye-opener about the future, and could help to revolutionise life here and now. It is also suitable for use by house groups, to provide vision for the new millennium.

'I welcome this clear and helpful discussion for several reasons, not least because it shows what it means to live as people who are grasped by hope.' STEPHEN TRAVIS

Tony is Rector and Patricia full-time Reader in the Anglican parish of Hawkwell, Essex, where they have pioneered a radical church development and youth strategy. They both have national ministries – Patricia as Director of Time Ministries International and Tony as Director of ABWON.

Hodder & Stoughton
0 340 71390 9

I Believe in Mission

Alistair Brown

For Christians the desire that others might also believe in Christ should be natural and instinctive, says Alistair Brown. For some, that will mean sharing their faith with family, friends, colleagues and neighbours. For others, the call to the unevangelised areas of the world will be powerful.

Whether called to share our faith at home or abroad, mission is the responsibility and privilege of every Christian. Mission is commanded by God, and is necessary if people are not to be lost. Mission also requires great passion: it's not merely spiritual scalp-hunting – it means caring for the whole person's needs.

This book is a biblical and practical call to mission. Only through radical, compassionate mission can the dream of a changed world be realised.

'This book is a real treat, all that a book about mission ought to be: inspirational, practical, funny, biblical, wise and readable. Enjoy it!' LYNN GREEN, YOUTH WITH A MISSION

Alistair Brown is General Director of the Baptist Missionary Society, and the author of *Near Christianity*.

Hodder & Stoughton
0 340 69427 0